W9-CLK-968

AFRICAN WRITERS SERIES

Editorial Adviser · Chinua Achebe

4

ZAMBIA SHALL BE FREE

AFRICAN WRITERS SERIES

Founding editor   Chinua Achebe

Kenneth D. Kaunda

ZAMBIA SHALL BE FREE
An Autobiography

HEINEMANN
LONDON IBADAN NAIROBI LUSAKA

Heinemann Educational Books Ltd
48 Charles Street, London W1X 8AH
P.M.B. 5205 Ibadan · P.O. BOX 45314 Nairobi
P.O. BOX 3966 Lusaka
EDINBURGH MELBOURNE TORONTO AUCKLAND
KINGSTON SINGAPORE HONG KONG KUALA LUMPUR
NEW DELHI

First published 1962
Reprinted 1962, 1966, 1967, 1969
1971, 1974, 1977 (twice), 1978

ISBN 0 435 90004 8

Printed Offset Litho and bound in Great Britain by
Cox & Wyman Ltd, London, Fakenham and Reading

Contents

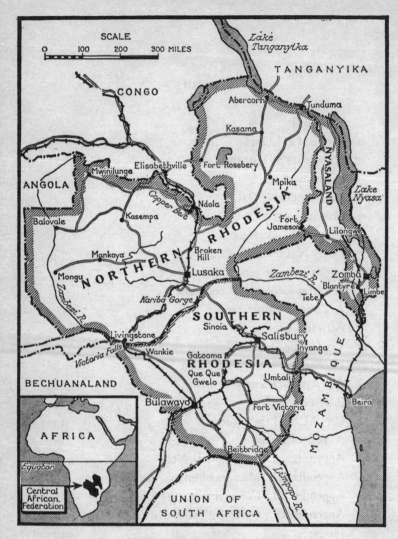

CENTRAL AFRICAN FEDERATION

FOREWORD

I have known Mr Kaunda for many years. The other day he introduced me, saying 'Here is Sir Stewart Gore-Browne, who has lived in Africa longer than I have'.

I first came to Northern Rhodesia fifty years ago and have lived at Shiwa Ng'andu for forty years. It is my home and that of my children and grandchildren. For nearly fifteen years I represented African interests in the Northern Rhodesia Legislature, a job which involved travelling throughout the length and breadth of the country. Mr Kaunda and I have always been friends, so if anything I can write will help him I am only too pleased to do so.

I have read his book and it represents very fairly his own point of view. What is even more significant, I think it is now fair to say that it represents the feelings of the great majority of sensible people, European as well as African, in Northern Rhodesia.

STEWART GORE-BROWNE

London
May, 1962

Boyhood at Lubwa

My parents gave me the name Buchizya, meaning 'the un-expected one', for I was born in the twentieth year of their marriage, the eighth in the line of children, three of whom died young. I was born in 1924 at Lubwa in the hills of the watershed between the great Luangwa and Chambezi rivers. My father, David Kaunda, was the first African missionary to be sent by the Livingstonia Mission of Nyasaland in 1904 to the Bemba-speaking people of the Chinsali District of Northern Rhodesia. For many years, he and my mother made their faithful witness among the Bemba, winning the confidence of the Chiefs and people. The Mission Station at Lubwa, eight miles from Chinsali, was not built until the pioneer missionary Mr McMinn came to join him.

My father died when I was eight years old and I cried bit-terly when I heard of his death, for I loved him and all my memories of him are sweet ones. He was a strict man, always expecting to be obeyed without question. He ruled his family with a firm hand but only once did he beat me. Until the day I die I do not think I shall forget that beating my father gave me. I was sore for days afterwards and he had to treat me with some soothing medicines. For an advocate of non-violence, this is not an edifying story to tell, but perhaps it was that early disapproval by my father that taught me not to fight with my brother man. It is so long ago that I forget now what the quarrel was about. All I remember is that I was very angry over something with the young son of the schoolmaster at Lubwa. He was just my age and for the first time in my life I went for him and in a moment I had him on the ground sitting astride him and rained blows upon his head. As luck would have it my father came by and saw me belabouring his colleague's son. That was the end of the fight and the cause of the beating, and each time my father applied his healing medicines, he rubbed into my small childish mind the wickedness of fighting. On only two other occasions in my life have I given way to violence but I must reserve those stories for later chapters in my life.

My father was for many years headmaster of the school but, in later life, he was ordained as a minister of the church. This responsibility meant that he frequently went off on tours round the villages visiting his people. My dearest memories of him concern the family hour before he departed on these tours. He would call my mother and my brothers and sisters and we would sing some hymns and he would pray with us. How I loved to sing with him. Indeed, my mother has often told me that as a very young child I would stand up on these occasions to imitate him as he beat time to the music. The sweet music of those hymns in the soft language of Bemba, my mother tongue, gave me my first love of singing which has never left me.

My father was a fine preacher, though I remember none of his sermons since, as a child, we always came out of the church before the preaching began. I think he must sometimes have preached sermons which did not please the

6

missionaries, because I have a vivid memory of once playing in the sand outside my father's house after a Sunday morning service, of being conscious that Father was sitting on the veranda at a table discussing something with Mr McMinn, Rev. Maxwell Robertson and Dr Brown. Suddenly I was startled by a loud bang and looking round I saw that it was my father who had thumped the table; he had jumped to his feet and was speaking animatedly to the missionaries.

Lubwa, set among the lovely hills of Chinsali in the Northern Province of Northern Rhodesia, was a good place in which to live. Old Mr McMinn, whom we called Shikulu – 'grandfather' – my own father and the other missionaries had created out of nothing a busy community of order and peace, which I look back upon with a deep thankfulness, realizing how much I owe to my early training in that place. Although we were five children in the family, I never remember sitting down to a meal with just ourselves present. There were always numerous guests and visitors in our home. During the term time there were always boys with us, sons of my father's friends who could not find school fees and whom my parents out of kindness had taken in. An early memory comes back to me of seeing some bowls of food set out in preparation for a meal, and while the guests gathered round they were startled by the sound of roaring in the forest near by. Someone laughingly said it was a notorious practical joker who could imitate the roar of a lion by vibrating a kind of root in a drum, but suddenly the roaring came nearer and no one could mistake it for anything but the roaring of a lion. Panic gripped everyone. My elder brother grabbed me by the hand and I was dragged along, hardly able to touch the ground with my scampering

7

toes, so eager was my brother to get me to the safety of a neighbour's house.

My parents could never have entertained so many guests and visitors in our home, on the meagre salary of a minister, had they not made big gardens for growing food. My mother made soap which she gave to those who helped with digging and weeding. Ten miles away they grew rice in a river-bed and not far from Lubwa they cultivated a large area of land. Their generous hospitality became famous and their home was known everywhere as Galilee – the place of peace and rest. The land in the Northern Province is very poor and the only way of getting a crop of any kind is by the system of *chitememe*. In the dry season, the men go out with their axes into the forest and, climbing the trees, they lop off the branches. These are then stacked in long piles and burnt before the coming of the rains. The BaBemba are the most expert tree climbers in Northern Rhodesia and there is great art in the way the branches are stacked before burning, for if they do not burn slowly and burn away completely, the soil beneath the fires is not sterilized and, when the seeds are planted in the ash, the weeds grow up and choke the millet. Only in this way has it been found possible to get a crop from the ground. There was no shortage of land to cultivate in the Northern Province and we did not kill the trees by lopping off the branches. Over the years, the bush regenerated and could be cultivated again. My people, through long ages of trial and error, had learnt how to live with Nature and win a living from the infertile soil.

After my father's death, my mother expected every one of her children to help her in keeping house and home together. Though I was a boy, I was made to do every type of work around the house and in the gardens. I learnt to carry water from the well two miles away – we were never allowed to make any excuse for not washing because there was no water – and my mother insisted on us stripping for a bath every day. I learnt to kneel by the grinding stone and grind the millet for the evening meal. I learnt to sweep and clean the cooking pots and wash my own clothes and iron them as well. There was firewood to be gathered from the forest and always work to be done in carrying poles to build the grain bins and the chicken houses.

My father had planned for me the best education possible which, at that time, could only be obtained in South Africa. He planned to send me as soon as I had received my basic education to live with Z. K. Mathews, but of course that was not to be. The method of teaching young children in the nineteen-twenties was to gather them under a tree on which was hung a cloth painted with the letters of the alphabet. I well remember sitting for hours under a shady tree chanting 'a-e-i-o-u', then forming the letters with my finger in the sand. We would smooth out a little area near where we were sitting and the teacher would wander round among the children correcting our letters. Each cloth was called *Nsalu* and when we had *Nsalu* one, two and three, we were promoted to the first class, when we were allowed to use slates. There was no free universal education at that time and every parent had to find half a crown a year. Just before my father died, I had been ill with influenza and so unable to attend the opening of the school. When I did at last present myself at school the teacher asked for my two and sixpence, and when I told him that I had no money, he sent me back to my mother to get the necessary half-crown. I ran sobbing to her, but she had no money in the house and she wept with me. Fortunately, a kind neighbour came to our aid and lent us the money which was in due course repaid. For so small a thing in those days could a child for ever forfeit the privilege of his life's education.

When I at last reached the stage when I was promoted to the middle school to take my Standards III, IV, V and VI, it was necessary to find school fees of thirty shillings a year. My mother had food in the garden to feed me and managed to scrape together enough to buy my clothes but I had to work in every school holiday for the fees. The Mission was kind enough to employ me at ten shillings a month digging ditches to drain the school garden and doing other jobs around the place. In this way, for three months of the year, I earned my school fees and in later life, when I became a teacher, it gave me a great sympathy for schoolboys who had to struggle to get fees for their education. Also at this early age I was learning the great value of self-help and as I shall relate in another chapter it led me to form the self-help club amongst the schoolboys at Mufulira.

At the age of nine, something happened which was to start me off on the road of instrumental music which has been one of the greatest joys of my life. A certain Eurafrican man, a friend of my brother, came to visit us from Livingstonia. He brought with him an 'autoharp' with twenty-one strings and three bars of music. He taught my brother how to make music with it and when he left he sold it to him. It was not long before I had persuaded my brother to teach me how to play this instrument and it was my constant companion during my leisure hours. We played the music which the miners brought back from the towns; it was the dance music of the West but we gave it our own rhythms and of course I soon began to compose my own airs and little songs. I can conceive of no more perfect relaxation after a hard day's work than sitting back in the light of the stars and the moon, playing my harp while my friends and companions danced to their hearts' content. When I became a teacher, I purchased a guitar.

As a boy I suffered terribly from sores on my legs and on my head. I also had frequent attacks of malaria. I was one of the best-known patients at the hospital where I went twice a day for treatment. Had it not been for the kind attention of the mission doctor, Dr Brown, and the missionary nurse, I should not be here now writing this book. It was at the hospital that I first met a boy called Simon Kapwepwe who became my firm friend and is now with me in U.N.I.P. as Treasurer-General. In spite of the sores on my legs, I became passionately fond of football. Our school Principal, the Rev. Maxwell Robertson, organized the whole school into village teams and I, of course, played with the Galilee team. We started very young, kicking a tennis ball around and it was not long before we were allowed a real football to play with.

It was as a result of one of these football matches that I was led into my second fight. We had beaten one of the other village teams in a football match but they would not accept defeat and after the match was over they challenged us to a fight. The other team was composed of much bigger boys than any we had in Galilee and they chose the biggest of them all, sending him out like Goliath from the Philistines to challenge one of our team. Our biggest boy was too unwell after the game to accept the challenge; the next we called upon could not face the ordeal and so the lot fell on me. Apart from that early fight with the schoolmaster's son, I had never learnt to fight at all, but I felt I had to do my best. It was not long before the other boy had me down on the ground. He came on me like a charging buffalo as I lay on my back but I met him with a tremendous kick in the stomach which sent him over backwards and in a moment I was up and sitting astride him triumphantly. Unknown to me he had a knife in his pocket which he drew out and started slashing me all over my scalp. When the spectators saw the blood they fled and I managed to disengage. I worried not at all about my wounds which were only superficial but I did not know how I was going to face my mother since my white shirt was covered in blood. I took it off and rubbed it all over with soil till it was so dirty no bloodstains could be seen and when my mother asked what had happened, I am afraid I lied to her and said it had been a very rough and dirty game. I do not think to this day that she knows about that desperate fight I was pushed into to uphold the honour of my team.

2

Schooldays at Munali

We were very fortunate in having a man of Maxwell Robertson's energy and drive as Principal of the school. Everything he did was conducted with the maximum of efficiency. Discipline was strict and no boy was allowed to be a slacker. He was the founder of the Boy Scout Movement in Northern

Rhodesia though, in those days, we called ourselves 'Path-finders'. Most of the boys in the school were in one or other of the scout troops and Maxwell Robertson deliberately cultivated the Scout spirit and loyalty to the troop to break down our tribal rivalries. No aspect of our education was neglected, mental, physical and spiritual. At that time, my mind was set upon following in my father's footsteps as a minister of the church. I think my mother from a very early age had kept this ideal steadily before me. The normal way to the ministry was by serving the church first of all as a teacher so, when I finished my Standard VI, almost as a matter of course, I was accepted into the Lubwa Normal Training Course for teachers.

For two years more I went on with my education in the Teacher Training Course and life was very little different from that of a schoolboy. Living in the Mission, I had started schooling at an early age, so I was one of the youngest of the teachers in training. I do not have any outstanding memories of that time except that once a number of us went on strike. The previous batch of students had completed their training in one year while our course was due to last for two years. For some reason we got it into our heads that we were being unjustly treated and we went on strike in protest. I cannot remember taking the matter very seriously, for after we had packed our blankets and gone off home for three or four days, we came trickling back to school and we were accepted again as students without even being asked to apologize.

In August 1940, the first Secondary School was opened at Munali in Lusaka and in 1941 I was chosen along with twenty-nine other students from schools throughout the territory to take my Form I at Munali. In all my life I had hardly set foot out of my own Chinsali District and now I was being asked to make the long trek to the town. It was my first long journey on a lorry and we came within an ace of having a serious accident. On the second day after leaving Lubwa the driver of the truck, who had been drinking heavily all the previous day, lost control of the lorry. The road was narrow and fortunately we were passing right through a place with high banks on either side where a cutting had been made through one of the great anthills which abound in our part of the country. The lorry hit one bank, swerved across the road against the other and came to rest in a cloud of dust. We were all very shaken but the shock sobered the driver and we drove on. At Mpika we found that we had missed our connection with another lorry going south and we had to wait four days kicking our heels with nothing to do.

I shall never forget my arrival at Kapiri Mposhi. I was then just seventeen years old and I had never seen a train. I don't know what I was expecting, but I was certainly looking forward to something wonderful when we reached the line of rail. I had been travelling for days with no opportunity to wash properly and I was longing for a bath. From my earliest childhood I had been accustomed to bath every day and to bath in privacy. Now I was shown a communal wash-place which was indescribably filthy. I hung around for hours trying to pluck up courage to go in and hoping against hope that some moment would come when I could have the place to myself. The lavatory was so disgusting, I could hardly bring myself to use it. It took me many days to get over the shock of that first arrival at Kapiri and I still shudder when I think of it.

Once at Munali, after those eight wearisome days of travel, I found myself in a new and wonderful world. For the first

14

time I saw a laboratory and we started to learn some real science. To begin with I was completely puzzled by the biology classes but soon the subject came to have a great fascination for me. I had never been good at mathematics but at Munali I had a good teacher and the subject soon lost its terrors so that when we took the final examination I came second in the class. History had always been my best subject but for some reason I did not do well in it, perhaps because it was all South African history that we had to study. English literature I came to love but I came down badly in the grammar paper at the end of my course.

We lived a full and interesting life at Munali. It was by no means all work and study in the classroom. I immediately found myself in the football team and we had many exciting and some very rough matches with local teams. I still carry on my leg a large scar where I was injured by the boot of one of the Lusaka 'Tigers'. Great emphasis was laid on athletics and I ran for my house in the mile and the half mile. In my second year, I led my house to victory in the inter-house athletics competition although I nearly lost the house the cup by my performance in the mile race. I led the field in the first and second lap but I must have started out at far too fast a pace because I was soon lagging far behind. Even though I was last in the race, I kept doggedly on and when I received the house trophy from the hands of Sir John Waddington, he gave me a word of commendation for having run the race to the end. I am glad that my first encounter with the King's highest representative in my country was a happy one. Not all my encounters with Governors have been so fortunate, as my history will show.

There was a good deal of bullying of the younger boys by

the elder ones and this greatly upset me. I was never bullied myself but there were only two of us in my year who managed by fierce argument with our persecutors to avoid having buckets of cold water thrown over us at times. In my second year, I was captain of my house with a small room to myself at the end of the dormitory. Many of the younger boys in the first year would come and hide in my room when ragging was in progress and I did all I could to protect them and discouraged any form of bullying in my own dormitory. I had learnt the value of strict discipline both from my parents and from Maxwell Robertson, and was determined to have the same kind of discipline in the school during the week I was duty prefect. My friends tell me that I used to march round that week with a set and serious expression on my face. I used to wear my hair with a parting on the right and my forelock brushed down almost over my eyes. This hair style coupled with my forbidding appearance when on duty earned me the name of 'Hitler'. However, I found it paid off well as the boys soon discovered that during my week on duty there were no detentions to be worked off on a Saturday. I also became quite popular with the masters who rarely found themselves called upon to punish anyone during my duty period.

The master who had the greatest influence upon me during my Munali days was Daniel Sonquishe. He was from South Africa and had taken a degree at Fort Hare. On a Saturday morning, all the boys were detailed off for special duties in keeping the whole place clean and some of us would go to help the masters in their homes. Daniel Sonquishe was a bachelor and I would frequently go to sweep his house on a Saturday morning. When I had finished work he would ask me to sit down and would talk to me about his life in

South Africa. For the first time I understood the meaning of the word *apartheid*. I heard innumerable stories of the indignities which my fellow Africans suffered at the hands of white men in the Union. Sometimes Sonquishe would say to me: 'Kenneth, it is almost too late for us to do anything about it in South Africa; we've lost our chance, but here it is not too late. Young men like yourself must make sure that what happened to us in the South will never happen up here. It is up to you now.' We all had a very great respect for Sonquishe. We knew that he was supporting a crippled father and that from his meagre salary of £13 a month he would regularly send home £10.

Perhaps the thing that brought us closest together was our common interest in the guitar. He and I formed a dancing troupe and at the end of my second year, in the school holidays we set off for a concert tour of the Copperbelt. We performed in most of the Copperbelt towns to good audiences, but the tour was not the financial success we had hoped for, as someone stole the greater part of our takings. I myself was in some difficulty because on the way to the Copperbelt I had lost my wallet in which was my government travel warrant to take me back to my home. When I got to Broken Hill, I went to see the head clerk at the Boma who was a friend of mine and asked him to come with me to see the District Commissioner to explain my predicament and ask for a new warrant. When I got into the office I said 'Good morning'. The District Commissioner turned to the head clerk and said 'tell this man in Bemba to say "Good morning, *sir*".' Throughout that interview, the D.C. insisted on his head clerk interpreting everything he said into Bemba while I spoke in English. After spending all my school days trying to become proficient in English and having studied

English literature, this D.C. wanted to push me back where he thought I ought to be – 'just an ordinary native'.

At Munali, we had a very active debating society which I joined. We were not of course allowed to debate any political subjects and I do not recollect much of what went on during our debates, though one incident stands out clearly in my mind. I had been asked to propose the motion 'That rats are found only in dirty houses'. I did my best with a subject which I did not really agree with; then just as I was sitting down at the end of my speech a big rat ran across the room and everyone started laughing and jeering. Needless to say when the motion was put to the vote my seconder was the only one to support me.

3

Schoolmaster

I passed my Form II examination and was one of the eight boys chosen to go on to Form III and IV, but teachers were so urgently required back at Lubwa that the missionaries called me home and I found myself appointed as boarding master of the Lubwa school for boys. Although I was glad to go back to my old home, it was a very difficult task I had been asked to undertake, for all the other teachers on the staff were very much senior to me, even though I had higher educational qualifications. Though I had completed two years in the Teacher Training course and done some practice teaching under supervision, I had never had any great responsibilities.

I think I was regarded as a strict disciplinarian, though at the same time becoming very popular with the boys because of my keen interest in football and my guitar playing. At that time, I took a very great interest in clothes. I had my suits and even my shorts specially styled by the tailor at Chinsali and the schoolboys began to copy the style in their own dress.

At Chinsali, the Government Boma five miles from Lubwa, the Chinsali African Welfare Association had been founded. Most of the members were Boma clerks and local teachers. I became a member. We discussed all matters relating to the welfare of Africans in the area. If we had any complaints to make we sent resolutions either to the D.C. or to the missionaries. My own interest was mainly on the social side of our activities. We organized dances and football matches. For many years I kept the minutes of those meetings, but long ago they were eaten by white ants and my only recollection of our business was an issue concerning the provision of boots for the district messengers. I cannot remember why we felt so strongly about this matter but we made regular complaints to the D.C. on the subject over a period of years and received no satisfaction.

Welfare Societies appear as a very early feature of African urban society. Professor Epstein in his book, *Politics in an Urban African Community*, described them as follows:

Welfare Societies were the subject of comment at a conference of District Commissioners held in 1936. The

D.C., Broken Hill, spoke of them as 'a representative body of educated native opinion'. At Broken Hill, the Welfare Association appears to have been treated as a kind of advisory board, and was consulted by the District Commissioner before he made his recommendations about new tax rates. When the new rate was announced, he again invoked the assistance of the association to explain the change to the general public. The same D.C. added that while the association undoubtedly represented 'the thinking and politically-minded Africans', he himself regarded it as 'an excellent barometer of native opinion'. Other speakers took a less favourable view of the Welfare Associations. One spoke of them as 'debating societies which give the educated native an opportunity to get up before his fellows and air his English'. The general opinion seemed to be that since the members of the societies were drawn from the educated class, and were mostly clerks and *capitaos* (foremen) they could not be considered representative of the African population as a whole. The feeling of the conference was that the associations should be allowed to develop along the lines of debating societies, but that they should not discuss political matters.

As early as 1945, my old friend Lt Col Sir Stewart Gore-Browne was pointing out the value of welfare societies which he set in contrast to the official Urban Advisory Councils. In a memorandum to the conference of Provincial Commissioners which met in 1945, he said that the reasons for the superior vitality of the welfare societies lay in the fact that when the District Commissioners nominated the members of the Advisory Councils, they were bound to select representatives from all the main sections in the community, whereas the welfare societies, which generally had

no formal constitution, merely attracted the most progressive
and energetic individuals in the local community.

This view was not generally acceptable to the conference
and the Provincial Commissioners stated that they felt that
the welfare societies consisted predominantly of the more
advanced and educated Africans, 'who represented no one
but themselves'. This fantastic statement underlines one
aspect of our long struggle for freedom. We who believe
that we are the mouthpieces of the inarticulate masses to
express their own feelings of frustration in a society domin-
ated by white settlers are branded as political agitators
giving way to personal ambition and lusting for power. As
late as 2 March 1960, Mr John Roberts, the leader of the
United Federal Party in the Northern Rhodesia Legislative
Council, warned the public against 'power hungry politicians'. He was of course referring to myself and my colleagues in U.N.I.P.

I spent four years as a teacher at Lubwa, busy not only
in school and with the Chinsali Welfare Association work
but with my pack of 'trekkers'. We could not call them
'cubs' because that was the name reserved for European
packs. Happily now the African 'Pathfinders' and 'trekkers'
are now united with Europeans in the Boy Scout Association.

Unknown to me at this time, my mother was giving long
and anxious thought to the problem of finding a wife for
me. Over at Mpika on the Great North Road there lived
the Banda family, who had been friends of my parents for
many many years. Mr Banda was a well-known business
man with a store near the Mpika Boma and he had a
daughter who, unlike most girls at that time, had remained
in school up to Standard IV. She was a hardworking girl

who earned a little pocket money by working as a 'nurse girl' for the D.C.'s wife during the hours when she was not in school. She was one of only two girls in the top class of her school and held her own with the boys. In 1944, she went to the famous girls' boarding school at Mbereshi to do her two years' training as a teacher. There she received her early training in cookery, dressmaking and other domestic science subjects.

With unerring judgment, my mother selected her from amongst all the other girls in the area as my future wife and the marriage arrangements were concluded between the parents. In June 1946 I was travelling to Mufulira for a Scout Training Camp under the leadership of the Rev. F. J. Bedford (now a secretary of the British and Foreign Bible Society in London) and passing through Mpika, my cousin arranged for me to meet Betty Banda. I had no doubt when I first saw her that my mother had made a wise choice and I have never had reason since. Betty has borne me six strong sons and at last a baby daughter, Musata, the joy of our hearts who, if she is not asleep, can hear the tapping of my typewriter as I write this book. It was many years before my wife became reconciled to my wandering life as a politician. I think she still wishes I was a respectable schoolmaster. Betty has been kept busy bringing up the family and I have not often been at home to help her. Once during the Congress days in Lusaka, she joined the 'Women's Brigade' and took part with hundreds of other women in a demonstration outside the D.C.'s office. The police dispersed the crowd with tear-gas. On that occasion, Titus Mukupo (now of the *African Mail*) who was watching the demonstration was arrested and jailed for eighteen months though he had nothing to do with organizing the procession.

Although I did my job as a teacher at Lubwa under John Nelson with efficiency and I think some enjoyment, I was restless. My brother was in the army, and on two separate occasions I applied to become a teacher in the Army Education Corps. The first time my mother dissuaded me, and the second time the missionaries persuaded me that my duty lay at home. Looking back on this period of my life, I ask myself why I was not content to remain a teacher. I had a good position and I was happily married. Although the salary was not majestic, I could get most of my food from the garden and most of my money went on clothes. I think on reflection that I was reacting against being tied to my mother's apron strings for so long and weary of the authority of the Mission. All my life I had done what others had planned for me and I wanted to break away and be on my own for once. I started to look around for other teaching jobs.

4

My Wandering Days

There were three of us, teachers at Lubwa, who were great friends; Simon Kapwepwe, from the days we had sat on the veranda of the Lubwa hospital waiting for our sores to be dressed, and John Sokoni. Simon and John had accepted a teaching post at a high school in Tanganyika. When they arrived there they were given a glowing account of their prospects and Simon wired me to come up and join them. I immediately caught the lorry to Mbeya but when I arrived I was greeted by two very disappointed friends. Their conditions of service had come through from Dar-es-Salaam and their hopes were dashed. We all three decided to go back home. On our journey through Tanganyika we saw a wonderful plantation of gum trees which had been planted only six years before and were already producing gum poles which were being sold at a good profit. The plantation was run by an African and his European friend. I well remember the three of us sitting on a hillside above Mbeya looking out over the lovely hills and discussing our future. We said that if gum trees could be grown in Tanganyika, they could also be grown in Northern Rhodesia. Had we not seen the great plantation at Shiwa? We realized that we could not start farming without capital so we determined to go to the towns to look for work that would enable us to amass enough capital to start farming. I still remembered that there were opportunities in the army for qualified teachers so Simon and I decided to go to Lusaka to apply. After some delay we were accepted and started work, but after only one day of service we were given half a crown and told to leave the work. I have never discovered what happened but I think news must have reached the army that we were 'undesirable' characters.

I had already applied for a teaching post in Southern Rhodesia so I travelled on to the south. It was a Salvation Army school near Salisbury. Unfortunately, my departure from Northern Rhodesia was delayed and I arrived late at the school to find that the post had been taken by another

With Frank Chitambal, my private secretary until 1961

With Sir Stewart Gore-Browne and Mr M. M. Temple

Addressing U.N.I.P. at Mulunguishi, July 1961

Seated, l. to r., Solomon Kalulu, Sikota Wina, Mainza Chona, self, Lewis Changufu and Nalumino Mundia

teacher. However, the head of the Mission said that there was a vacancy at another school some 85 miles from Salisbury at the Bindura Mine. I had little alternative but to accept this appointment, so I duly boarded the bus and set off. I well remember my thoughts on that painful journey. I had been travelling for five days with never an opportunity to take a bath; I was tired and dirty and in a strange country without friends. All my thoughts were of home and the parable of the Prodigal Son was never far from my mind.

As we neared our destination, the bus drew up at the side of the road and looking out of the window I saw an old woman filling a calabash from the muddy trickle of rainwater in the gutter by the roadside. I asked my companion what this woman could possibly be doing, for it was the rainy season and she could hardly have wanted to water her garden nor could she be carrying water to make bricks. My companion showed no surprise at what seemed to me such extraordinary behaviour and said that there was little water in this part of the country and that the woman would have to walk miles to the nearest river. She was drawing water, he said, for ordinary domestic purposes.

I must have presented a strange sight to the eyes of the headmaster of that school when I stood on the doorstep of his house. I had a bulky rucksack on my back, a large box of books, a suitcase of clothes, a bundle of blankets on my head and my guitar over my shoulder. My hair was full of dust and my clothes were dirty and crumpled. The first thing I did was to ask where I could wash. I was told that the river was three miles away but that there was a place down the road where water could be obtained. I set off and after some time I passed a filthy pond where cattle up to their knees in mud were drinking. I went on, keeping my eyes open for the place where I could wash, feeling more tired, more hungry, more dirty with every step. After what must have been a mile and a half walk, I asked some people passing by where was the place to wash. They directed me back to the cattle pond. I had no alternative but to walk back along the road and do the best I could to cleanse myself in that wretched place. When I finally got back to the school, I was given a meal that was so badly prepared that I could hardly choke it down. That night, I determined to get back home as quickly as possible but in the morning I realized that I had no money left. There was nothing for it but to sell something. I thought of my precious guitar but its music was my only comfort in those days and I could not be parted from it. I had bought a second-hand jacket from Mokambo on the Congo border for thirty shillings, which I managed to sell for fifty, and a sweater my mother had given me I sold for seven and six, though it was worth a great deal more.

I got back on the bus to Salisbury. The ticket clerk there would not sell me a ticket until I had produced a 'pass'. It was the first time in my life that I had been asked to produce a pass and, of course, I had none. Who could have issued me with one? I knew all about Southern Rhodesia's reputation for harsh pass laws and I had visions of being arrested on the spot. Frantically I put my hand into my breast pocket to find my Northern Rhodesia identity certificate which I must have known had no validity in Southern Rhodesia but which at least showed my name. By a stroke of luck, my Church Removal certificate from Lubwa lay alongside my identity certificate in my wallet. I pulled it out and before I had time to make any explanations the ticket clerk took this official-looking document for some kind of pass and

My mother, self and wife, with our only daughter

With my sons Tilyenji, Masuzgo, Kaweche and Wezi

My present house in Chilenje – Hut No. 394 from which Zambia African Congress was launched

Government House, Lusaka

gave me my ticket without asking any questions. After buying my ticket, I counted my small change and found I had exactly three and sixpence left for food. I bought a loaf of brown bread and a bottle of Mazoe Orange Crush. Knowing that I had a four-day journey before me, I took out my knife and carefully divided the bread into four equal pieces.

At Bulawayo I saw my first fight between a European and an African. The African was a cripple, lame in both legs and the European was punching him in the face. Although the African was a lame man he had powerful shoulders and powerful arms. Suddenly turning on his assailant, he grabbed him by the wrists and began to shake him as a dog will shake a rat. I was afraid that something terrible would happen, so I rushed to where I had previously seen a policeman, but he had gone and when I came back the fight was over. Some bystanders had parted the two men. This was the first and only time I have ever seen a real fight, with the exception of the cowboy fights I have sometimes seen on the cinema screen.

When I boarded the train again at Bulawayo, I found myself sitting with a family travelling up to Kitwe on the Copperbelt. We chatted together and when I pulled out my bottle of Mazoe, I offered them all a drink. We became quite friendly and they must have noticed that all day I ate nothing but my small ration of brown bread. That evening they offered to share their meal with me and I accepted their generous hospitality, but all next day I avoided them, being embarrassed that they should expect to have to offer me food again. What a relief it was to cross the Zambezi once more and arrive back in my own country. There I met some of my former pupils from Lubwa who took me off the train and gave me a bath and food. The Prodigal had returned home again.

Still looking for capital for a farm, I went to the Copperbelt. When my friend John Sokoni had left us after the Tanganyika trip, he had gone to work in a shop at Kitwe. I thought I would look him up and see what luck he had found as a shop assistant. I met him on the pavement outside the shop. He was coming out with a long face. He had just been given twenty-six shillings for a month's work.

Although I did not realize it at the time, I now nearly fell into the hands of the World Federation of Trade Unions. There was a certain European, leader of the European trade union on the mines who, much against the wishes of his white brothers, was advocating that Africans should be brought into the (European) Mine Workers' Union. He had just come from an overseas conference of trade unionists where he had been offered a sum of money to help him organize the bringing of Africans into his union. I applied for a job as an organizing secretary of this African branch of his union but, for a reason I did not know at the time, the scheme was dropped.

It was only after reading Professor Epstein's writings which give an account of the formation of the African Mine Workers' Union that I learnt the story behind this episode. This is worth relating for it illustrates our African suspicion of any overtures made to us by white settlers:

> The possibility of a strong and independent trade union movement among the African mine workers was viewed by the European miners as at once representing a serious threat to their own position. The President of the (European) Mine Workers' Union, who some time previously had said of the formation of African trade unions that one

could not stop a mass movement, began to make overtures to the Africans, whom he addressed at a number of meetings. He sought to persuade them to drop the idea of forming a separate union and instead to enter the existing Mine Workers' Union. He argued that the African union would be weak and ineffective since, being sponsored by Government, the Africans would not be accorded the right to strike. He pointed out further that such a move would strengthen the position of the mining companies by causing a division in the ranks of labour. However, these advances were rejected by the African leaders. Why was it, they asked, that no such proposal had been made in all the years that had passed since the (European) Mine Workers' Union came into existence, until the Africans appeared to be about to have their own union? The African leaders claimed too that if, raw and completely inexperienced in trade union affairs, they went in with the European miners, all executive control and power to conduct negotiations would be vested in the whites. The Africans asked how, if they were not to have responsibility in running their own trade union, they would be given the opportunity of showing that they were capable of shouldering responsibility in the wider political sphere.

This was how I narrowly escaped being a trade unionist. I now realized that having been trained as a teacher, my best chance of earning capital was in teaching work. I applied for a teaching post on the Copperbelt. While I was waiting to hear whether my application had been approved, I got a job as a Welfare Assistant at the Nchanga Mine. My salary was £4 per month and I was terribly bored. All I seemed to be asked to do was to hang around the Welfare Centre and open up the library. Nearly all the books in the library I had read when I was at school, and my boss was a man for whom

29

I had no respect. It came as a relief when I was accepted for teaching again. By this time, Betty and my firstborn child had joined me and we went together to Mufulira. I was appointed as boarding master of the school under the management of the Rev. Fergus McPherson and my wife taught in the primary school. We determined to work together to improve our standard of living and in order to increase our combined income (I was earning £5 13s. 6d. per month and my wife £3 3s. 6d. per month), we decided to buy second-hand clothes from Mokambo, just over the Congo border, and send them up to my home to be sold at a small profit. People were permitted by law to cross into the Congo to buy second-hand American clothes, but each person was only allowed to bring back one jacket and one dress or shirt. At the end of the month when I had received my salary, I would organize a group of schoolboys and on a Saturday afternoon we would cross the border at Mokambo and come back wearing the strangest assortment of clothes.

Many of the boarders at the school had difficulty in finding their school fees, so I organized them into a self-help club. They bought seeds and made gardens near the school to grow vegetables. These I bought for the school instead of going to the market. In this way, a number of boys earned their school fees. Some of the older boys wanted to join the local branch of Congress, of which I was Vice-Secretary, and in order to raise their subscriptions, they agreed to bring along each a penny per week which I collected. I took great delight at Mufulira in training the church choir, and it became quite well known.

I was chosen by the other teachers to represent them on the Urban Advisory Council. I served on this Council for a long time but the meetings were very dull. Its members were nominated by the D.C. after consulting with the various groups represented in the Council. In 1949, I was elected to go to the Provincial Council and only narrowly missed being chosen by that body to represent them on the African Representative Council for the whole territory.

5

Colour Bar

In Mufulira, for the first time, I found myself suffering the indignities of the colour bar. Africans were not permitted to enter the European shops by the front door. If they wanted anything, they had to go to a hole in the wall at the side of the shop to ask for it. I determined to expose this system for what it was, an insult to my race and my people. I told some of the boys in the school that I intended to challenge the colour bar and I chose a certain chemist's shop in town which was notorious for its treatment of Africans. As well as medicines, this shop sold toys and books. While my boys waited outside on the pavement, I went inside and asked politely for a book. I remember it was Arthur Mee's *Talks to Boys*. My friend John Sokoni had once rescued a tattered copy from a miner who was using its pages to roll his cigarettes and it is a book that has had a profound influence on my life.

The girl behind the counter had probably never been addressed before by an African in her own language. She motioned me over to the chemist who stood behind the counter. I repeated my question. Pointing to the door, he said viciously, 'Get out of here.' I said again, 'I am only asking for a book and I can get it nowhere else in town.' He said, 'You can stand there till Christmas and you'll never get a book from me.' I was just thinking that as it was the month of August I would have to wait rather a long time, when two white miners in their overalls walked into the shop. Hearing the proprietor say again, 'Get out,' they took me by the arms and frog-marched me to the door. There they were met by seventeen angry schoolboys who objected strongly to their schoolmaster being treated in this manner and they said so in no uncertain terms. A vigorous slanging match followed in which we were called 'black-skinned niggers' and we replied by asking what was so wonderful about a white skin anyway. Being so heavily outnumbered, the two Europeans made for their car and made a quick getaway.

I immediately went round to the Boma to make a complaint about the way I had been treated. There was a young District Officer there whom I knew well. He took me into his office. He listened with sympathy to my story and began thumping the table in his indignation. He said, 'Look here, Kenneth, if ever you want anything just come along to me and I will give you a note.' 'But,' I said, 'that is not the point, what about all the thousands of others who want to be treated like reasonable human beings in the shops? Have they got to come to you every time for a note?' He promised to write a letter to the chemist and I let the matter drop. A few days later, I decided to go into the shop again to see whether the District Officer's words had made any difference. Again I made a simple request but it was a different man behind the counter and he ordered me out of the shop. I said that I would see to it that something would be done. He just laughed scornfully and said, 'You try.' I again went round to the Boma and this time the District Officer accompanied me back to the shop. I distinctly remember him saying to the chemist, 'Do you realize that you have been behaving like this to a man who may before long be sitting in the Legislative Council?' (It was just at the time when I had been elected to the Provincial Council.) The proprietor was a little taken aback and asked me into his dispensary to apologize. He said, 'Mr Kaunda, if only you had told me who you were, I am sure I would not have ordered you out of my shop.' Once again I had to explain that I was not asking for any special consideration for myself, I was simply asking that my people should be treated with reasonable courtesy in their own country. I left Mufulira soon after this incident. No one else followed up my protest and things reverted to normal in the shops.

I never challenged this issue again until 1957 when I was visiting Kitwe with Harry Nkumbula, President of the African National Congress. This being the white area of Kitwe there were no African eating houses near by. We drove to a café, having been told by our driver that this café would sell us what we wanted, provided we did not demand to take our meal there; but he did not tell us that even to do that we had to stand by the door where an African servant could come and ask us what we wanted and could then go in to get us whatever we wanted. We went into the café to the counter and I asked for some sandwiches. In reply a young girl of about seventeen told me that 'boys' were not served at the counter. When I told her that I was not a 'boy' and all I wanted was a dozen sandwiches, she spoke to an elderly white woman who was apparently in charge. On asking me what I wanted, she repeated that 'boys' were not served at that counter. I repeated in my turn that I was not a 'boy'. At this point I was dragged out of the café by my clothes by a European man who had already dragged Harry Nkumbula outside the café. This white man hit Harry and called him a cheap, spoiled nigger. Five other white men joined him in attacking us and we defended ourselves. White men and black men passing joined in the fight, and an *apartheid* type of brawl took place. This was my third and last fight.

We were ordered to leave the premises but we refused on the grounds that the white men who had started the fight could get away if we did so. In the end we were given an escort of an African policeman despite the fact that we were the complainants. The white men went to the Charge Office unescorted.

At the Charge Office we were asked to make a statement. Harry Nkumbula began by saying that the girl at the counter refused to serve us. Before he could end his sentence, the white superintendent of police who had come to stop the fight said, 'You cannot call a white lady a "girl" or a "woman".' Harry ignored this and went on to say that 'after that an elderly woman came . . .' but again, before he could finish his sentence, the superintendent said, 'I say, you cheeky nigger, you cannot call a European lady a woman.'

Then this police officer called Harry to a room and closed the door and beat him up. Harry told this officer that he was lucky he was wearing Her Majesty the Queen's uniform, or one or other of them would have been killed.

34

When the case came to court, our demand that we should be medically examined by a doctor chosen by us was refused and we therefore chose not to continue with the case.

The following morning after the incident a group of mine-workers went to the café and said to the proprietor, 'We have heard that our leaders were beaten up here. We have come to have our revenge.' There was a police guard on the café and the leader of the group of men was arrested and fined.

This was the type of incident that was taking place con-tinually in the Federation which, according to spokesmen like Sir Roy Welensky, was achieving racial partnership and good feeling.

Even as I write, in spite of the passing of anti-colour bar legislation by the Northern Rhodesia government, unfor-tunate incidents can take place. This very month (March 1962) the Vice-President of the Christian Council of Northern Rhodesia, the Rev. M. S. Lucheya, entered a café with his European colleague, the President of the Council, and was refused a cup of tea. Can anyone wonder that we sometimes feel bitter about the European settler who treats us like some kind of subhuman species in the land of our birth?

Of course one could fill all the pages of this book with stories of this kind. Amongst ourselves, we spend hours laughing about these things because they often make the Europeans look very silly. In our U.N.I.P. headquarters, we have an office orderly who is a faithful servant of the nationalist movement. He is a small man who has never had the advantage of a good education so does not speak very fluent English. One day some years ago he went to the old Lusaka post office which, at that time, was segregated. Un-wittingly he found himself in the European side and as there were not many people about he went up to the counter and, pushing a shilling under the grill, he said, 'Please penny stamps madam'. She did not take any notice so, trying again, he said, 'Please penny stamps girl.' At this the assistant called a policeman and our orderly was asked to explain his behaviour. In his own forceful way he said to the policeman, 'Me say stamps madam. She nothing. Me say stamps girl. She nothing. Me say this thing stupid.' Fortunately the policeman had sufficient sense of humour to laugh it off.

6

I Decide to go Home

The decision to go back home was reached by the three of us, Simon Kapwepwe, John Sokoni and myself, late in 1948. We saved up to secure bicycles to enable us to move about and attend meetings freely. We decided to purchase watches in order to be on time for such meetings. My wife and I decided we should also get a sewing machine to help us to repair whatever second-hand goods I could bring back from Katabulwe that needed to be mended before selling. I have already mentioned my week-end trips to Mokambo. The small savings from our meagre monthly pay packets, plus what we managed to raise from the sale of these second-hand goods helped us to purchase our three main requirements.

I remember how we were thinking of what we were going to do for a container for our belongings when the biblical teaching of Jesus Christ came out strikingly, 'Therefore take no thought, saying, What shall we eat? or, What shall we drink? or, Wherewithal shall we be clothed? . . . for your heavenly Father knoweth that ye have need of all these things.' One morning Mr Nkaka, who was a good friend of our family, came in to see us. He told us he and our senior boys were in the process of making us a wooden trunk for our clothes. It was quite a relief for us and we made our sincere thanks known to our friend. Mr Nkaka was head instructor at our school and he and Mrs Nkaka were also members of our church choir. This kind of incident, of which there have been many in my life, have helped me immensely and given me encouragement.

A good number of our friends came to the Mufulira railway station to give us a send-off. In spite of the fact that our school boys and girls were on holiday, there was quite a crowd to see us off. At Kapiri Mposhi we looked in vain for the Kapwepwe family, who were to join us there, so we left without our friends. We did not have sufficient money to enable us to pay our personal fares as well as transport for our few belongings, so we paid for my wife as far as Mpika Boma, where my parents-in-law were then living, and paid for Sokoni and myself and our bicycles up to Lukulu, some ninety miles south of Mpika Boma. We got to Mpika safely the following evening after a restful night at Lukulu. We were wondering how we would cycle through the lion-infested areas between Mpika and Chinsali, some one hundred and twenty miles, when our faithless hearts were once more reminded of how providential the Creator is. On that day, one of our friends who was driving a lorry offered us a lift to Chinsali. We got back home to a big welcome. Sokoni went home to his parents and I remained to plan what I would do next.

Many old friends came to welcome us home and among them one of my very early friends who had disappeared for a long time from our district and who had come back during my own absence. He was Robert S. Makasa who was still teaching at Lubwa. For the first time in my life I was sitting down to plan my life my own way.

I was caught up immediately by three things. There was the farming instinct, the trading in second-hand goods instinct, and the political one. As a firm believer in the co-operative movement where people are poor, I got some few friends together to open up a co-operative farm at my own mother's place. We called it the Chinsali Youngmen's Farming Association. Sokoni started a similar one for the area south of us. We were both made managers of our respective places. I must say we did very well in view of our having no prior experience. We read extensively anything we could lay our hands on about agricultural science. These were very happy days for me. I had the satisfaction of planning something and realizing it on my own. We then had only one child, Panji Tushuke. This is the boy who, on his first birthday, in my presence and that of a good number of my pupils, got up and ran to the wall and never went back to crawling again. That is how he began to walk. He did not want to miss me and I always had to sneak off when going away, for he would always follow crying and calling me back if he knew I was leaving him. All my former school-boys at Mufulira remember and ask after him when I meet them, for he was very popular with them. I built myself a four-roomed house and a very well laid-out front garden.

My senior sister who had retired as a nurse also came to live with us and we built a four-roomed house for her. My brother, who was still teaching, lived in his old three-roomed house when he came on leave, and my second sister shared her sister's house with her when she came back on leave. We were a very happy family group.

I grew a good number of vegetables. My one-acre orchard consisted of orange, lemon, guava, pawpaw and mango trees. There were also bananas. My one big difficulty was irrigation. One of my greatest pleasures was in rearing chickens. My neighbour, a very hard-working farmer called Aaron Mbalashi, reared some improved stock. He sold his improved stock of eggs at fourpence each and in this way he helped us all to improve our poultry. Then there were our maize, cassava, bean, corn and other fields. The most enjoyable period was when seeds were germinating. All this meant real hard work but it was all my own and I simply loved it.

There were the second-hand goods which had earned themselves the name of Mokambo. I suppose this was due to the fact that most of the first popular second-hand goods were found on the Copperbelt and were bought from Mokambo. I would cycle for over three hundred miles up to Katabulwe across the Luapula River in the then Belgian Congo with some of our neighbours and we would cross the Luapula back to Northern Rhodesia and then would come the scramble to load them on the Thatcher and Hobson goods' lorries. All this was terribly strenuous. And then came the long race cycling home to try and arrive back before our goods. During my absence from the farm, my sister took charge of the farm labour and my wife dealt with the second-hand clothes shop.

My political activities did not end with my leaving the

39

Copperbelt. Late in 1949, I contacted the General Secretary of the Northern Rhodesia African Congress, who then was Mr Robinson Nabulyato, for permission to open up a branch of Congress in Chinsali. I got the authority to go ahead and then discussed this with Makasa and Sokoni. We agreed that the best way of going about it would be to introduce this to the Chinsali African Welfare Association. We did so and Congress was given a cautious welcome in Chinsali. Early in March, Makasa was elected Chairman, I was elected Secretary and a friend of ours, Mr Simon Sula, was elected Treasurer. We learnt later that news had gone round that taking office in Congress meant going to prison. This rumour was so strong that the nominations were in actual fact arranged to use us as guinea pigs since we had ourselves introduced Congress. Mr Sula was head accountant at the training school while Makasa was headmaster of Nkula Lower Middle School.

The period that followed was one of the most amazing in my life. During the week, I would be working at my farm while Makasa would be teaching. On Fridays, I would cycle to his school and then after work we would cycle for distances of from forty to sixty miles. We would be singing hymns which the Rev. R. D. McMinn and Rev. P. B. Mushindo translated into Bemba from the Church of Scotland hymn books. We placed ourselves, more than ever before, entirely in the hands of our Creator. Chinsali District has always had plenty of man-eating lions, but whether such man-eating lions were at large or not was immaterial. We went on and organized our people. When Makasa was too busy to go, Sokoni was usually there, and when neither of them was available, which was rare, I went alone. What was the message that the Chinsali people were receiving at this time? We had to make our people conscious that they were human beings just as good or as bad as any other. Even twelve years ago this message was not difficult to put across to our people. I was aware that most of our people who had gone to fight in defence of the British Empire had suffered for nothing; we were only employed as hewers of wood and drawers of water, and we could not eat from the same tables nor share the same beds in hotels. I would ask which was more important: to prepare someone else's meals and beds or to share them? Was it not common sense that a person who prepared your meals and made your bed and looked after you was controlling your life? How stupid it was for anyone to say you may control my life but I will not sit at the same table with you because you are stinking or because you are black. Then there was my most popular story.

This was the story of an African soldier who was not even called a soldier, but an *askari*, and yet sent to fight against Hitler, who was a horrible racialist. In fact, we went to defend the so-called Western or Christian values. I would point out the differences that existed in pay, uniform, food and in all other conditions of service. I would then portray this *askari* demobilized with none of the promises made to him fulfilled. This *askari* would suffer so much, he would end up a road labourer. Then he would ask for a lift from his road foreman who would put him at the back of a Government van while his dog shared the front seat with him. At an hotel, the Big Bwana would leave him to look after his luggage while he himself went in to take a meal. The dog would be given some food while this ex-*askari* would have nothing. Then they would arrive in town and this man, who risked his life just like his English counterpart, would go to a shop to see inscribed above the door, NO

41

DOGS ALLOWED INSIDE. To his surprise when window-shopping he would see an actual dog right inside through the window. On his attempting to get inside he would be met at the door with a big, *'Get out of here, you nigger, bobojana'* (meaning monkey). *'No Kaffirs allowed in here.'* Then would his own fellow black man come to order him out. *'Tata kabiyeni kunse uko ku ntolokoso ekushitila abafita muno mwa ba bwana epela.'* This means, 'Go out to the pigeon-hole. Only white men may come in here.' Then this ex-*askari* would look back to the days before the Second World War. He would remember how campaigns were conducted to recruit him, and others like him, the differences between a black and white serviceman, the promises he had been given of what could be done for him on being demobilized. Then he would come nearer to where he was: how his road foreman exposed him to the heat, the cold or the rain, while he shared the warmth and all with his dog. He would end up asking, 'Where is the partnership in this country that Welensky talks about?' From there on he would decide to join the Northern Rhodesia African Congress. This is how almost all my meetings were addressed. I would end up by asking whether what I was saying was true or not true. Someone courageous enough would stand up in support. A good number of ex-servicemen found themselves weeping with the speaker, so did many members of the audience, both men and women. What I said could not fail to be effective because it was what the African experienced and, to a very large extent, still experiences today. The difference is that while in 1950 fewer people realized what was happening was wrong, more do so today. Now people realize, by the thousand, not only that what has been happening is wrong but also that, if they come together, they can remedy the wrong.

In this way I warmed up Chinsali to a comparatively high level of political consciousness.

Mr R. R. Stokes, who was so impressed with our efforts to organize ourselves as farmers that he helped to develop our area by opening a new road from the Boma to the Lubu plains, was one day tackled very seriously about his sympathies with us. It was the first time there had been such a direct conflict between a representative of the Crown and the common man. This took place at Senior Chief Nkula's village. I don't remember what the trouble was exactly but this man found courage to speak and he spoke. I can well remember the expression of utter disgust on the Government officials' faces.

In 1951, something happened that helped to hasten the pace of African nationalism in this country. Mr Harry Nkumbula, who was on one of his trips to the Indian Ocean islands to collect sea shells for sale in Bwila, was invited by our then General Secretary, Mr Nabulyato, to attend our conference in Lusaka. Mr Mbikusita was then our President. I remember that among the things he said was:

> I believe that the future of the African people of Northern Rhodesia is safer in the hands of the Colonial Office than it would be under any form of responsible Government or Federal rule. I do not believe that the Colonial Office would exert such a strong influence if Northern Rhodesia was amalgamated to Southern Rhodesia, which has almost full responsible government.

Speaking of representations made to the Secretary of State, he went on:

> It is not only on the fair-mindedness of the individual

Minister holding that office that the Africans rely. The Minister is answerable through the House of Commons to the people of Britain and the majority of these people – the voters of Britain – are working men and women who understand the troubles and hopes of working people in the Colonies better than the employers of those people, even if they live in Africa. The working men and women of England know what fair and liberal treatment has done to improve their lives and they will not grudge to Africans the same treatment.

Mr Mbikusita at this time was anti-Federation, as the following quotation shows:

You will remember that two years after the Victoria Falls Conference, I, as your President, addressing the Kitwe African Society, put forward a suggestion that a Federation between Northern Rhodesia, Nyasaland and Tanganyika would be more acceptable. It is unfortunate that the terms of reference of the London Conference were too narrow to include this suggestion. I would like, once again, to put this idea forward and include this time that Conference of delegates of all East and Central African States sponsored by Government be assembled in London to consider the need for closer association. Africans of this country and of Nyasaland would feel less anxious in a Federation which included the Mandated Territory of Tanganyika, the politically progressive country of Kenya and the African Protectorates of Uganda and Zanzibar. The influence of Southern Rhodesia's 134,000 Europeans would not be felt with the same force in so great a Federation.

He ended by praising Dr Hastings Banda and 'all our outstanding individual members'.

This is how the man who, in 1951, led the opposition to Federation ended his address and who in the following year was the first African to join the party that stood for Federation and has been in the Federal Parliament ever since. This is the story of the man who, in 1951, proposed a Pan-Africanist form of federation but the following year embarked on the way that has led him to oppose everything Pan-Africanist and to propose and fight for the secession of Barotseland from the rest of Northern Rhodesia. From here, another man took over from him.

7

Harry Nkumbula as Leader

I first met Mr Nkumbula in 1944. We travelled on the same lorry from Kapiri Mposhi to Shiwa Ng'andu. I had a vivid memory of him because at Mpika Boma one of our fellow-passengers took seriously ill, but the driver did not seem to care and, in fact, was preparing to leave the poor passenger behind when Mr Nkumbula surprised us by speaking very strongly to the driver, pointing out that it was his responsibility to see that the passenger was cared for. Drivers in those days, especially those who drove passenger lorries, were virtually kings unto their own. So for anyone to dare to challenge the king in his own domain needed great courage.

Seven years afterwards, I recognized Mr Nkumbula and reminded him of this performance and I remember Mr Nabulyato remarking that some people have good memories.

There were twenty-seven of us at this conference. Makasa and I came from Chinsali. Mr Nkumbula spoke against Federation for over an hour and he won our sympathies immediately. Meanwhile, some serious canvassing was going on. Mr Gordon Chindele was going round saying that if Mr Nkumbula was elected, he would mislead us as he was too hot-headed and that we should elect Mr Mbikusita and then make Mr Nkumbula an organizing secretary. I remember how furiously we worked to counteract what we thought was a wrong choice, even though I doubt if Mr Nkumbula knows to this day who his secret campaign agents were. Our efforts were rewarded when Mr Nkumbula received twenty-four votes, Mr Safeli Chileshe, who had just left government service as a teacher received three, and Mr Mbikusita received one. This shows that even Mr Chindele did not vote for his candidate, or else the candidate forgot to vote for himself.

In February 1952, we held a very explosive conference and it was at this conference that I met a white Northern Rhodesian who seriously treated Northern Rhodesia as his own country. He was a full member of the Congress and did not hide the fact. He spoke freely against Federation. I remember how moved I was by the speeches which he delivered in a very high-pitched voice. I had a feeling he was not safe at all. His political activities included the formation of an anti-Federation committee in Ndola. He, together with Reuben Chitandika Kamanga, Justin Chimba and Alick Chifunda were co-editors of a very inspiring Freedom

46

Newsletter which led to his being watched even more. One other thing I remember was when Mr Nkumbula who was speaking in reply to a threat from the Attorney-General spoke so inspiringly, I shouted, 'Long live Harry. . . . Death to the traitor.'

One other important thing that happened at this historic conference of February 1952 was the formation of the Supreme Action Council. This was a sort of War Cabinet on the lines of Sir Winston Churchill's. The Executive Council was left to deal with ordinary matters but the Supreme Action Council was to direct the fight against Federation. I was a member of this Council and our first meeting was held on 27 February. The Attorney-General reacted very sharply to our plans and issued threat after threat. The result was that the Supreme Action Council issued a public statement which was signed by Mr George Kaluwa, the then Vice-General Secretary. The statement said:

After a meeting of the Supreme Action Council of the Northern Rhodesia African Congress at Lusaka on 27 February 1952 the following statement was made by the General President to the open Congress and Congress endorsed it:

'The Supreme Action Council wishes to draw the attention of the public to a warning conveyed to the Congress by the Attorney-General through the two African members of the Legislative Council in the following words: *I am warning you that the Government will not hesitate to use its powers to deal with disorders caused including general strike planned by your meetings.*'

When the African members of Legco protested that the forcing of Federation was the cause of the tension, the Attorney-General said that it did not matter if the Government was good or bad; it was there to govern and it would do so.

The statement went on to say that no disorderly conduct was intended by Congress, and that Congress's protest action had been forced upon Africans 'by the refusal of the Government of the U.K. and of N.R. to pay any attention to the unanimous opposition' against Federation.

The conference came to an end but the atmosphere was not helped by the Attorney-General's threat. We were so upset that almost all delegates bought red ties to signify we were prepared to die for our country. All of us went back to report to our branches the important resolutions passed by the conference, one of which was to send a powerful delegation to Britain to protest against Federation. This was to be led by Mr Nkumbula and consisted of the Paramount Chief Chitimukulu, Senior Chief Musokotwane, Mr Nabulyato and the late Mr L. C. Katilungu. There was great enthusiasm in the whole country. Senior civil servants spoke at fund-raising public meetings. Committees to raise these funds were formed right through the country. The campaign went well and our delegation left. Thousands of pounds were raised and, looking back now, it is clear to all of us that we did not have the machinery to make sure that all the funds reached the Congress and so we must have lost thousands. This difficulty is one which faces many political parties including my own and we were looking into this seriously last year when disturbances began. We have now secured the services of a chartered accountant to help us devise methods of controlling the raising of funds.

Back at home, the agenda of all our public meetings now included our fight against Federation. We were fortunate to

8

Secretary, Northern Province

conference that I was appointed Organizing
the Northern Province. The Northern
at time, included today's Luapula Province.
s, I was charged with the responsibility of
people from the boundary of Serenje and
s to the Tanganyika border in the north, and
Nyasaland border to that of the then Belgian
west. All this had to be done on a bicycle. It
dous challenge and I was quite happy to
y', a wonderful training ground. Later, as
ral of the African National Congress and as
eral of the banned Zambia African National
d now as National President of the United
ependence Party, I am still able to draw on my
eriences of those days when I was a field

y difficult work, I had much help from a good
es. There was the inspiration I got from my
g of Abraham Lincoln's life; there was Arthur
s to Boys. Thanks are due to our friend and
ambai Patel who had, at that time, got us so
ture on the Indian struggle for independence. It
very first trip that I came to be introduced to
no never leaves my bookshelf and is always with

have the document prepared by Mr Nkumbula and Dr Hastings K. Banda when they were good friends in London. The document was very detailed and it was a great help to all of us who had copies and, in fact, it was reproduced at a later stage in pamphlet form. It is reproduced in full (pp. 166–76) to confute those who repeatedly say that we had no adequate reasons for rejecting Federation. Most of our grounds for rejection are still valid today.

And so the great movement rolled on. We had just received notification letters to attend the second session of the Supreme Action Council when news reached us that our white Congress member had been arrested. It was a very depressing time for most of us. Mr Mbikusita, our former President, gave evidence against this man, his former member, Simon Ber Zukas. I don't know what the charge was but Simon Zukas was deported to Britain. I am glad he is now happily married and settled. He is running a good business, a firm of civil engineers, and I do hope that we will be able, as a country, to benefit by his experience. I might add here, as a matter of interest, that a white supporter of ours asked me at a meeting in Luanshya what we would do if some of our white or brown supporters or members of U.N.I.P. were deported by the Federal Government. In reply I said that deportation would only be temporary and very soon we would be giving them a hero's welcome.

Our Supreme Action Committee, which met at Broken Hill in April 1952, was not a very happy affair at all. Some members did not turn up. Perhaps I should mention here that this is the time I posted our terribly angry letter to the missionaries at Lubwa which I refer to elsewhere. At this juncture, a friend of mine from whom I had taken over at Lubwa Training School, and who was in charge at Kasama

Upper School, suggested to some of our people who were organizing themselves as the Kasama African Welfare Association, which later they changed to Kasama African Institute, that it might be a good idea if they invited me to speak at one of their meetings on the subject of Federation. This man is Mr Henry Chibuta, now Assistant Manager of Schools at Mpika. However, this was not to be for, just at the time they were trying to contact me, a conference of Chiefs and people was called in Lusaka. It was a big affair. The London delegation reported back. It was all a most spirited occasion. Chiefs and their people mixed freely and stood as one in their opposition to Federation.

The Northern Rhodesia Government did not take all this very well. The Minutes of this conference carry this record:

Chiefs' Interview S.N.A.: The Secretary for Native Affairs, through the District Commissioner, Lusaka, sent two District Messengers to ask the African National Congress to allow the Chiefs to see him on 23 August 1952. The Chiefs debated the invitation and resolved that they accept it.

On 24 August, at 3 p.m., the Chiefs met the Secretary for Native Affairs. A full report of what happened had not been written but the Secretary for Native Affairs said the following in an interview with the Chiefs:
  1 You Chiefs should not surrender your Power to the African National Congress. The Congress is aiming at taking away your chieftainships.
  2 You should not subscribe money to the Congress, as it will only buy motor-cars with it and nothing else you will see done for you.
  3 A certain Chief refused to co-operate with the African National Congress; he is a very wise Chief indeed.

50

me on any trip I undertake; that book is *In Tune With the Infinite* by Ralph Waldo Trine. My family was also a great help to me. They did not complain that I was away most of the time. In fact, at one time I went away for three full months and brought back a beard. I was on the move all the time with the result that I did not write a single letter back home. Although they did not complain, they did discuss my movements between themselves – my mother, sister and my wife. They wondered whether I was just trying to dodge my farm responsibilities. This 'conspiracy', carefully concealed from me for some time, is now a source of great laughter when we remember it in our family.

To put down my experiences in the twelve months I went round the Northern Province would need a separate volume and so it must wait. But so much now has been said about my encounter with a lion that I think I should tell it here in my own words. In those good old days, teachers were not barred from holding office in the Congress and so I stopped at Mundu Lower Middle School where my old classmate Ason Charles Bwalya was headmaster and was also Branch Chairman. I addressed a meeting that evening. Early in the morning, I set off for Isoka Boma where I was scheduled to address a public meeting that evening. I had a very worried mind, a mind that was expecting something bad. I had gone about five miles when something passed me at a terrible speed and I almost fell off my bicycle since my mind was already in a frightened state, only to see a young smiling boy in front of me. Mr Bwalya had sent him to bring a pair of my heavy boots which I had left at his school. From there I tried to force myself to dismiss this fear by thinking it was all imagination, but the weight of foreboding was still there at the back of my mind. As I pushed my bicycle slowly I heard some noise from my left and then saw just about five feet in front of me a big lizard running faster than I had ever known lizards to run and close on its tail a big snake. I applied my brakes firmly and threw my bicycle down, but by the time I had done this the two had already gone. I started going on, more dragging myself than pedalling. I had gone about a mile from this place when I began to go uphill. To make matters worse, there was far too much sand to be able to ride and just after a bend, I saw from a distance of about a hundred yards what looked like a big monkey. It jumped from the north bank on the road and had obviously not seen me. The time must have been about eleven in the morning. It stood still for a moment or two and then moved on to the middle of the road. It quickly took a glance in both directions and it saw me and I realized immediately that my four-legged friend was no monkey, but a lion. To my great surprise the fear that had been haunting me quickly gave way to a feeling of strength and boldness. The beast stared at me as I advanced towards it. I must have been about twenty yards from it when I stopped. It continued to stare at me without making the slightest movement. I rang my bicycle bell and shouted but it still stood still and stared at me. It was of a fine brown colour and the mane showed clearly that it was full grown. I took my cycle pump and hit almost every part of my bicycle but the animal did not even wink as far as I could see. I don't know why, but all of a sudden I lifted my heavily laden bicycle as if to cross a stream without a bridge and waved it over my head with both my hands. This was too much for the King of Beasts; he made one leap and disappeared as quickly as he had come. I put my bicycle down, walked on and as soon as I left the sandy part of the road, I rode it once again to arrive in time for my Isoka meeting.

In this way I went round the Province meeting Chiefs, village headmen, teachers, traders, farmers, clerks and the ordinary members of the public. Wherever I could, I formed branches of the Congress. In August 1953, I was elected Secretary-General of the African National Congress and moved to Lusaka.

9

Secretary-General of Congress

During 1953 we continued our battle against Federation with a petition to the Queen in April, signed by one hundred and twenty chiefs. Seeking her intervention we wrote:

> We need your protection until there is a Government in this country in which we shall feel safe. . . . We can see that the Europeans are trying to bring us under the same domination as our brother Africans in Southern Rhodesia and South Africa; and to hold us there for ever as cheap labourers without hope of progress. We cannot accept this for our children. . . .

We added a note to this petition which stated that the Paramount Chief of the Barotse had not accepted Federation but had agreed not to contest its imposition provided the Protectorate status of Barotseland was assured.

Enclosing this petition, we wrote to the Speaker of the House of Commons, and the Lord Chancellor of the House of Lords, pointing out that among the signatories to the petition were the legal successors to those Chiefs who originally entrusted our territories to the Government of the United Kingdom. We drew attention to the fact that in the referendum conducted in Southern Rhodesia which had declared in favour of Federation, the white population, numbering 128,000, had approximately 49,000 voters on the electoral roll, while the African population of nearly 2,000,000 had 429 voters on the roll. Also, in the Legislative Councils of Northern Rhodesia and Nyasaland, to whom the question was next referred, there were only two Africans in each Council in memberships of 23 and 18 respectively. All the African members had voted and spoken strongly against the scheme. We went on to declare that the imposition of Federation would be contrary to the United Nations Charter and especially to Article 73 of that Charter and we appealed for a hearing at the Bar of the House of Commons or by Select Committee of both Houses of Parliament.

As everyone knows, our appeals went unheard and the time arrived for elections to the Federal Parliament. In my press communiqué of 13 October 1953 I said:

In Central Africa a major constitutional change has been imposed against the expressed wish of some six million Africans in favour of a handful of reactionary white settlers. This imposition has only been possible because the imperialists count on the strength of the British troops which they are ruthlessly using in crushing down the national aspirations of the colonial peoples. Nay, they have not solved the problem. They have only managed to shelve the inevitable racial strife in Central Africa. Serious trouble lies ahead. The imposition of Federation has made this trouble more certain than ever.

Nevertheless, we decided to co-operate in these elections. In the same communiqué I wrote:

> If we Africans are decided to continue fighting against human injustice, we will be well advised to link up our national movements with the established foreign parliamentary system. We must see to it that more and more of our men find their way to the parliamentary institution whilst on the other hand we intensify our national aspirations.

We were afraid that if the African organizations boycotted the elections the Federal Parliament might change the constitution after Federation so as to enable Governors of each territory to nominate African stooges. So, far from being defeated by the imposition of Federation, we called Congress to ever more vigorous action. At this time I was sending out regular circulars to Branch officials in which I did my best to encourage our people for the long struggle that I knew lay ahead of us.

But much of the time our struggle was misunderstood and our actions misrepresented and this has led to great bitterness and often to disturbances such as those in the Gwembe Valley, Luapula and the Northern Province, where Congress was blamed for stirring up trouble which arose from other causes. The Congress organizer regarded himself honestly as a worker in the cause of freedom and a means through which the frustrations of the people could express themselves.

The 'common man' of Zambia had no member of parliament to whom he could make his complaints when he felt he was being unjustly treated. He found himself being swept along in the current of change brought about by the coming of the settler to his country. His old safe world was falling in ruins about him and in his bewilderment he had nowhere to turn to. Congress regarded itself as the means through which African people could express their legitimate aspirations.

On the other side, the Government, in the person of the District Commissioner and his staff, regarded the 'Congress man' as a trouble maker who was trying to thwart all he was trying to do for the betterment of the people he had been sent to work amongst. Under the system of Indirect Rule, the Provincial Administration (i.e., District Commissioners and District Officers, collectively known amongst us as the P.A.), carried out its work through the local Chiefs and their Native Authorities. The African National Congress could not qualify as a political party because the mass of Africans were not voters and it came to be regarded as a kind of subversive organization whose object was simply to cause trouble. The Central Government dare not ban the organization because that would have caused such a rumpus overseas, so they tried to deal with it through the Chiefs and the Local Authorities. Some day, I should like to write a book with the old Congress files at my elbow to tell the wretched story of how the Provincial Administration tried to use the Chiefs to crush Congress in the rural areas.

In order to illustrate this I have included (pp. 186–96) the full report on the disturbances in the Gwembe Valley. It is a terrible story of misunderstanding and oppression. What the well-meaning, imperialist D.C.s have never understood is

With my wife singing Christmas carols at home 1961

Myself at Chilenje

that Africans are people, not cattle to be herded together and driven here and there. When the bewildered rural people did not immediately do all the things that the D.C. wished them to do for their own good, he decided to force them into goodness by Native Authority Orders. I know from my own experience that the people of Zambia are ordinary human beings with prejudices and fears but with intelligence and a great longing to improve their position. With patience and understanding, people can be led into a better land and the Canaan of their dreams, but they will fight back if you try to push them faster than they want to go.

I do not by any means put the blame on the D.C.s personally. I know many of them are good men and I count some as my friends; but they are forced to carry out a system that sets them into opposition to the very people they are supposed to guide with a fatherly hand. For example, at the time of the imposition of Federation, the D.C.s and the D.O.s had to travel round their districts to persuade the people to accept it. Some D.C.s have told me they did this very unwillingly. If a man is to become a friend to the people, to lead them to better things, he must know their language, yet the Central Government has a terrible record of shifting their Provincial Officers from one language area to another, never giving them time to lead and guide. For example, the Chinsali District, where the worst troubles happened in 1961, has had nineteen changes of District Commissioners and District Officers in ten years.

10

A Time of Frustration

During 1954, I realized that some constructive thinking would have to be done if Congress was going to hold together. People were saying that now Federation had become an accomplished fact, we could never break it and therefore we had no reason to continue our fight.

We decided to draw up a five-year plan and, accordingly, I sent out a circular in which I said that the past three years had seen a wonderful fight against Federation. The only good thing about Federation was the unity it had brought amongst us, and now people must learn that although Federation had been imposed upon us, this national movement to advance Africans politically, economically and socially must go on. All our efforts had been thrown into the fight against Federation. Now what next? Our five-year Development Plan would be launched officially on 1 September 1955. I concluded the circular with an appeal for support and for advice.

Later in the year we discovered that although we lived in what was called a Central African Federation, as Africans we were restricted in our movements. When Harry Nkumbula and I arrived in Salisbury to attend a meeting of the four African members of the Federal Parliament who represented Northern Rhodesia and Nyasaland, we were each issued with a deportation order at the airport. We were called

Alien Natives. How can you be an alien if you are also a native of the country? I have this order before me as I write. It is headed:

Order for the Expulsion of an Alien Native from the Colony of Southern Rhodesia in terms of Section 2 (1) of the Deportation of Aliens Act: (Chapter 61).
and states:

KENNETH DAVID KAUNDA

WHEREAS I deem it conducive to the public good that you, who are an alien, should not remain within the borders of the Colony of Southern Rhodesia,

Now, therefore, under and by virtue of the powers conferred upon me by the Deportation of Aliens Act (Chapter 61), I do hereby direct that you do leave the Colony aforesaid within one hour of the service upon you of this order.

R. C. TREGOLD.
Officer administering the Government.
Dated at Salisbury this 20th day of August 1954.

Mr Nkumbula's warrant of expulsion from Southern Rhodesia dated as far back as March 1953. Mine was issued on 20 August 1954, only four days previously. This seemed strange to us since Mr Nkumbula had been down to Salisbury during July the previous year and was not arrested.

We felt very bitter about this and, in my next circular, I commented as follows: 'It is anyone's guess to see the main reason why they didn't touch Mr Nkumbula that time – Federation had not been imposed as yet; now that it is, what have they to fear?'

The European press in Northern Rhodesia constantly

refers to the destructive forces of an exclusive black nationalism. Yet in September 1954, at the same time that I was writing so bitterly about Federation, I was preparing for Congress a scheme for an Inter-Racial College in Northern Rhodesia. The first Non-Racial College of Adult Education is in process of being built as I write this, seven years later.

As the year went on I drafted further resolutions addressed to the Secretary for Native Affairs and continuously strove to improve our organization. In my work as Secretary-General of Congress, I had been conscious for a long time of the need to have our own newspaper. Late in 1953, it was decided by the National Executive Council that a newspaper would help Congress both for propaganda work and as a source of income. An editorial board consisting of Titus Mukupo, W. K. Sikalumbi and myself was formed. The major problem, of course, that we faced was lack of finance. We went round all the printing presses in Lusaka but, of course, their estimates for printing a paper were far above anything we could afford. We decided to produce a cyclostyled monthly paper, *Congress News*, the first copy of which appeared in October 1953 at a loss.

Shortly after the second issue in November, both the President-General Mr Nkumbula and I were arrested for printing a newspaper without registering it. The Criminal Investigation Headquarters were, however, not aware that the Postmaster-General had been written to by us and had replied saying that he could not register it since it was roneoed and not printed. When we explained this, we were released but forbidden to publish our paper again 'until further notice'. This 'further notice' was not squeezed out of the authorities until we had got some friendly members of Parliament to bring pressure to bear on the Colonial Secretary.

We frequently issued press communiqués which were not always accorded much attention. In view of all the talk that is going on as I write this, about the possibility of splitting up Northern Rhodesia, I think it is worth recording that as early as 1954 I gave my reasons for rejecting any kind of partition by showing the obvious impracticability of the Van Eeden plan for separate African and White States.

If accepted, the Van Eeden partition plan would have meant a complete defeat of the still possible integration of men and women of different colours – a principle towards which men and women are struggling in many parts of the world today. So we fought the Van Eeden scheme tooth and nail and I'm glad to say it was never seriously countenanced.

Early in 1955, I went to prison for the first time. The events which led up to this are worth relating because they show that the authorities, which were hounding our organizers in the Provinces, were determined to get some of us at headquarters behind bars. Their opportunity came when they discovered that we held some prohibited literature in our office.

For some months, we had been receiving from a member of Parliament in London, copies of a magazine, *Africa and the Colonial World*. A request came that our statement in the Gwembe disturbances should be published in this magazine and, of course, we agreed. Unfortunately, the editor of the *Central African Post*, Frank Barton, who was later to become my very good friend, saw a copy of this and raised a hue and cry with the result that this magazine became a 'prohibited publication'. I wrote to the British member of

Parliament asking what we should do with the magazine since we had been sent a number of copies for distribution. He replied that we should send them to Southern Rhodesia where the publication had not been banned. I realized they ought to be disposed of so I bundled the whole lot up and put them on a shelf in the office. I scribbled on the wrapping a note to the effect that they should either be sent to Southern Rhodesia or taken to the Urban District Commissioner, Lusaka, to be disposed of, then I forgot about them. On 6 January 1955, shortly after I returned from a long tour, I was in bed when my wife woke me and said two Europeans wished to see me. I thought they were press men so I got up, put on shorts and vest and went out, and a European asked me to go to his car. As we walked along he said, 'Kenneth, we are asking you to go to your office.'

He was carrying a blue piece of paper and said he had a warrant to search my house, but that we should go to the office first.

At the office one of the white men read me a blue paper to the effect that he had the right to search. He asked me and I said I had no objection. Sikalumbi, the Deputy Treasurer, was also there. We got inside and the search began. One of the white men went to where the packages were, found them, and appeared to be satisfied. Next, my table was searched and a big envelope addressed to Mr. G. Kaluwa was found and put in a suitcase belonging to a European. Before that, Mr Nkumbula, who was President-General of my organization, had arrived with other white men and asked me if the packages were still there. I said, 'Yes, unfortunately, I have not been able to deal with them.'

Mr Nkumbula and I were sentenced to two months' imprisonment with hard labour.

1955 was an unsatisfactory year from the point of view of Congress activity. I spent much of my time on organization but it was difficult to maintain the enthusiasm of our branches. A number of our organizers in the Provinces were jailed for various offences. I tried to set out for our members the reasons for joining our movement, and sent out the following circular:

Your membership of the African National Congress, entered now, will help make possible
    the fight for the franchise;
    the fight against colour discrimination in public places like post offices, hotels, rest rooms, eating places, theatres, parks, playgrounds and many others;
    the fight to get Africans safeguarded against the prevailing police brutality and unlawful arrests;
    the fight for getting higher posts for Africans in the Protectorate's and Federal Civil Services, and in military and police forces according to merit and not according to their colour;
    the fight for better treatment of our Chiefs in the way of allowances as we declared at the August 1952 Conference and to stop all intimidation and ill-treatment of Chiefs and their Native Authority servants by Government officials;
    the fight for more and better educational and health facilities and to fight for free economic progress of Africans both in urban and rural areas;
    the fight against the establishment of a common native policy for the Federation;
    the fight against the final stage of this dreadful monster Federation which is intended to be a Central African Dominion, in other words the fight for remaining a Protectorate under the direct control of the Colonial

Office until we are ready to participate fully in the running of our Protectorate's affairs;

in short, all the above mean the fight for self-guards and not safeguards by someone else!

Once again, we say to you join now and give today and become a member of this national movement. If you join, you add yourself to some 105 Chiefs, 500 Native Authorities' servants, 3,000 village headmen and 37,000 men, women and children. You become a member for as little as:

Ladies	6d.	entrance fee,	1s. 6d.	annual subscription
Men	1s. 6d.	,,	,, 2s. 6d.	,,	,,
Students and				
children	3d.	,,	,, 1s. 0d.	,,	,,

But you may give us as much as you like!

During this year, the Government increased the pressure and a Bill was introduced into the Legislative Council to amend the Public Order Ordinance. We held two big meetings at Kabwata to protest against this Ordinance. The first one was held before the Ordinance became law, but obviously the authorities were beginning to take more notice of what we were saying at these meetings, because six white men led by a Welfare Officer attended the meeting. The second meeting was attended by two uniformed policemen. Of course, as the years went by and our organization grew in strength, policemen always attended our open-air meetings and took down what we said on tape recorders.

But it was not the police at our meetings which caused us most concern at this time. All the power of the press and radio was turned on to discredit us. A small incident illustrates this. In Government Communiqué 118 of the African News Service which was distributed to the press and to all

African reading rooms, it was reported that a well-known member of the African National Congress had been sent to jail in the Northern Province for four years for setting fire to a store at Chinsali. In fact this man, Kosam Mwamba, had never been a member of Congress. In one of my circulars I exposed this deliberate attempt to discredit us, and said that we hated violence and believed that it did not pay.

The Government did not like the things we were saying and yet they did not dare to silence us completely, so they employed their usual methods of working through Chiefs. For example a motion was introduced into the Ilamfya Council, which is composed of Bemba Chiefs, to the effect that African politicians should first get permission from the Chief before holding a meeting in any Chief's area. Some government officials who attended the meeting spoke in favour of the motion, but it was heavily defeated.

The Bemba representatives opposed the motion on the ground that European politicians are permitted to hold meetings in any part of the Colony, without obtaining permission from the Government. I learnt from a very reliable source that the motion was brought to the Ilamfya Council, the supreme Council of Chiefs in LuBemba, by one of the Chiefs who had been persuaded to do so by the D.C. himself. This Chief twice refused to take this motion to the Ilamfya Council but on the third occasion reluctantly agreed.

Perhaps because of the ever-increasing support Congress was receiving from the masses of Africans from all walks of life, Government was angered and, who knows, perhaps a little frightened too. I said at the time:

We want to remind people in authority that WHEN PEOPLE UNDERSTAND A CAUSE, BECOME PREPARED TO SUFFER

FOR THAT CAUSE AND SEE GLORY AND HONOUR IN SUCH SUFFER-
ING, IT IS INDEED JUST IMPOSSIBLE TO SUPPRESS THEM OR THE
CAUSE THEY STAND FOR. More and more Africans are seeing
the cause this Congress stands for as right, and so are add-
ing themselves to it. In view of this, our best piece of New
Year advice to Government is this; that the best way of
destroying the African National Congress is not by banish-
ing it violently but by removing as much of what forms
Congress's platform as they can possibly manage, and
plenty can be done, for is not much of our racial conflict
brought about by colour discrimination? Does this colour
discrimination not bring about frustration and confusion
in the minds of the victims? Don't they see that once they
get together, speak and act as one, some good might result?
Africans, like any other human beings, are refusing to
allow anyone to make their colour the basis of discrimination against them. They no longer will allow anyone to
make them third or fourth class citizens in the country of
their birth.

We wish to draw the attention of Government to this
important fact that once they banish Congress, they shall
have succeeded only in driving African nationalism under-
ground; and, as every thinking person knows, under-
ground movements are not pleasant movements for anyone anywhere, and it is our sincere hope and prayer that
people in authority will not abuse their privileged positions
for the temporary satisfaction of one section of this multi-
racial society.

During 1955, we who had almost given up hope of any
encouragement from white Liberals were delighted to find
Dr Scott, the Federal member of Parliament for Lusaka,
championing the same cause as ourselves. I gave full promi-
nence to his statements in one of my Congress circulars, and

emphasized that Dr Scott had, both in and out of Parliament, pressed governments in Central Africa to adopt a more liberal attitude towards the indigenous people. His appeals had fallen on deaf ears and instead the privileged class and legislators had raised more and more oppressive legislation in an attempt to stop the indigenous people demanding their legitimate rights. I pointed out that we were preserving patience and appealed once again to the leaders of the privileged classes to do something about the 'many wrongs that are committed against us on grounds of colour, before our people lose patience'.

By 1956, our African National Congress was getting down seriously to work out the kind of constitution we thought fitting for our country. In view of Zambia's rejection of the 1958 constitution imposed by Lennox Boyd it is necessary to give in detail our own proposals, and these are contained in Appendix (III, p. 176).

We also made suggestions for a revision of the Federal constitution, in a *Memorandum on the failure of the Federal government to provide higher education for Africans and of the Northern Rhodesian government to provide secondary schools*. In this memorandum we pointed out that the Federal government had reduced the number of grants and scholarships provided in the past for overseas higher education of Africans, and that it was the wish of Africans that the question of their higher education should no longer be an item of Federal legislation, but should become a territorial item. While Uganda had more than 200 Africans doing university courses in the United Kingdom, Northern Rhodesia had only about ten receiving any education there. This was particularly surprising when the revenues of the two countries were compared.

We went on to complain that the multi-racial character of the Rhodesian university had been departed from in planning to house European and African students in separate hostels. Furthermore, several South Africans had been appointed to the staff of the university, but no African had been appointed.

On the question of the provision of candidates for the university, we stressed the need to extend and develop secondary schools. There were no African secondary schools for girls, and it appeared that there would be no African women in the university for many years. The only junior secondary school for girls was at Chipembi Mission. In fact, the education of girls in Northern Rhodesia was so much neglected that nearly all the African hospital nurses and trainees were from Southern Rhodesia.

As far as technical education and training was concerned, progress was so slow that Africans found it difficult to take advantage of the agreed plan for advancement in the mines and in other branches of industry. The memorandum ended, 'If the government of Northern Rhodesia has the principle of *Partnership* at all at heart it must give Africans the same opportunity and standard of technical education and training as the Europeans. There is no apprenticeship scheme for Africans in any industry in Northern Rhodesia. Africans are explicitly excluded from the terms of the Apprenticeship Ordinance. (See Cap. 187. Laws of Northern Rhodesia Section 3, 2 (a).) The mass education of adults, of great importance to a community seeking a fuller franchise, has been allowed to die out for lack of government support and enthusiasm.'

African Opinion

When the Second World War ended, the question of the further industrial development of Northern and Southern Rhodesia became a matter of urgent concern. It was essential that full use should be made of the large rivers for the production of electrical power, as well as for purposes of irrigation.

In Northern Rhodesia, the plan which met with most support was for the harnessing of the Kafue river, not very far from the point where it flows into the Zambezi, so that electrical power might be produced, and the fertile land irrigated farther up the river. In Southern Rhodesia, the idea was to make use of the Kariba Gorge, through which the Zambezi river flows.

By the time the question of Federation began to be seriously considered, the Northern Rhodesian Government had already spent considerable sums of the taxpayers' money on the preliminary works required for the Kafue scheme, such as the construction of an approach road. Sir Godfrey Huggins, then prime minister of Southern Rhodesia, was believed to have given an undertaking that the acceptance of Federation would not be allowed to interfere with the Kafue plan which was expected to be of such great benefit to Northern Rhodesia.

However, later on when independent French experts were

called in they declared for the far more ambitious and much more costly Kariba scheme, and little more was heard of the Kafue. This may well have been the correct decision under the circumstances, but at the time a good deal of ill-feeling was aroused in Northern Rhodesia. Business men in Lusaka were particularly bitter about it.

On 17 November 1955, acting on the instructions of the Executive Council of Congress, Mr Nkumbula sent a petition to the Queen on behalf of the people of the Zambezi Valley, who were being dispossessed of their land to make way for the Kariba Gorge hydro-electric scheme. It was pointed out that the whole of the land within 200 miles upstream of the Kariba Gorge, on the Northern Rhodesian bank of the Zambezi was either Native Reserve, or Native Trust Land, and as such was set aside 'for the sole use and benefit, direct and indirect, of the natives of Northern Rhodesia'. The Queen was asked to instruct the Secretary of State for the Colonies to consider fully the security and well-being of the people of the Zambezi Valley, who were living under Her Majesty's protection. He should determine, for example, whether it was just that the people should be dis-possessed of their land, and whether the Kariba project was for the benefit of the natives of Northern Rhodesia. The question of compensation to be paid to the 29,000 people of Northern Rhodesia, and 14,000 of Southern Rhodesia, who were to lose their homes, was also mentioned; and the suggestion was made, that a Commission be set up to examine and determine the various points raised. As everyone now knows, the Kariba project was quickly carried through, and resulted in the formation of an enormous lake, completely swamping the area above the dam, which had been the home of thousands of Africans for many generations.

African opinion in Northern Rhodesia, completely flouted on the Kariba project, was unable to make itself properly felt even in smaller ways. In urban areas, opinion was supposed to be voiced by the urban Advisory Councils. To these, Africans were elected on the ward system, and the Council was presided over by the local District Commissioner. These Councils had no executive functions. They met once a month to consider a prepared agenda when matters of local interest and complaints and grievances were considered. It was then for the District Commissioner, if he thought fit to do so, to take such action or make such representations as he considered to be necessary. He was their sole mouthpiece.

For the remedying of the grievances of the great African consumer population in the Protectorate, the Advisory Councils have proved useless, and the only body which was prepared to put up a serious fight in the interest of the African consumer was the Congress. We in Congress in 1953 started a militant campaign of protest against *apartheid* in the post offices and the shops. Ignoring all notices to the contrary, we invaded shops and post offices in large numbers and soon forced the abolition of segregation.

There was a trader at Kasama in Northern Eastern Rhodesia, who had a chain of stores through the district. We received numerous complaints about his treatment of African customers. They were, it was said, bullied, ill-treated and insulted. He was said, on one occasion, to have caused the death of an African. Congress instituted a boycott which was so effective that, after enduring it for some months, the trader sold out. His successor was more amenable; peace was made and there has been no further trouble. Our Congress organizer, Makasa, however, went to jail for 18 months for organizing this boycott. The year 1956 marked a campaign of boycott in most of the towns in Northern Rhodesia. In all the cases, before commencing operations, Congress sent a letter to the local Chamber of Commerce mentioning its complaints and asking for a conference at which these complaints could be discussed and remedied. In every case, the answer the Chamber of Commerce gave was that it was not prepared to meet the Congress or its leaders, but that grievances, if they existed, could be handled by the local Urban Advisory Council. Our answer was to refuse to accept this position, and boycotts which followed were almost uniformly effective as far as African consumers were concerned. In Chingola, after a boycott had started, the local Chamber of Commerce agreed to meet the local branch of Congress. A conference was held and the boycott was at once called off. In refusing to recognize or meet the Congress, the Chamber of Commerce, composed entirely of European and Asian traders, were, we understood, following a lead given to them by the Northern Rhodesian government.

The European and Asian bodies of traders did not take the boycotts lying down. Complaints were made to the Government, and whatever action was considered possible was taken against the boycotters. In the Kasama case for instance, three or four of our members were convicted of conspiracy and sent to prison for long terms. In most of the other local boycotts, individual pickets, or the more zealous enforcers of the boycott, were sent to prison on charges of assault or intimidation.

Matters came to a head at Mufulira on the Copperbelt in May 1956. The local committee wrote to the Chamber of Commerce on 23 May setting out a substantial list of grievances felt by the African consumers, and asked the Chamber to meet it. The Chamber sent a reply refusing to meet the

committee but expressing its willingness to meet the local
Advisory Council. We refused to accept this position and a
boycott commenced on 11 June, being, so far as the African
customers were concerned, 100 per cent effective. This time
the protests of the commercial community stirred an apparently reluctant Government to action. A prosecution for
conspiracy was instituted against the two leading members
of the local committee, the Deputy Provincial President, and
the senior Provincial President for the Western Province.
This fourth man, Edward, Mungoni, was arrested by the
police in Lusaka, handcuffed to an African constable,
marched through the streets to the railway station, taken by
train to Ndola and there, similarly handcuffed, again
marched through the streets on several occasions. This unnecessarily harsh treatment acted, as it was bound to act, very
considerably to exacerbate African feelings on the Copperbelt.

On this occasion, we decided to fight. We engaged the
services of a senior member of the Salisbury Bar, and the
matter was heard before the magistrate of Mufulira on 3 and
4 July. The case for the Crown was that the conspiracy was a
malicious one, inasmuch as all legitimate grievances which
the African consumer population were labouring under
could have been remedied through some official channels
upon their being represented to the African Advisory Council
of Mufulira. Stress was laid upon the fact that the first three
defendants in the case, who were the principal officials of
the African National Congress in Mufulira, were also members of the Urban Advisory Council of that town. Therefore it was said, when the Chamber of Commerce refused to
meet the local African National Congress, it was not actually
refusing to meet these three persons as it would have met

them in their other capacity as members of the Council. This being so, it was argued there was no substance in the complaint that the African National Congress had been ignored and, therefore, the calling of the boycott was malicious. It was called, so the Prosecutor said, not in the legitimate protection of consumer interests in Mufulira, but in pursuance of a campaign to enforce recognition of the African National Congress.

No attempt was made by the principal Crown witnesses, who were the D.C. and the Secretary of the Chamber of Commerce, to deny the existence or validity of the grievances set out in the Congress letter of 23 May. After the boycott started, price inspectors went to Mufulira and three of the twenty-four European tradesmen there were convicted of overcharging or giving short weight. In the butchers' shops meat was wrapped into parcels at specific prices, and African customers were expected to buy these parcels without knowing, or being given an opportunity of knowing what was in them. Any African who insisted upon opening the parcel before buying would receive short shrift.

Forty-pound bags of mealie meal, which is our staple food, would be delivered to European customers free of charge, but Africans would be expected to take their own delivery, though prices were the same. The hatchway system, under which Africans were not allowed into shops but had to take their purchases through a small opening on to the street, had mainly disappeared throughout the territory, due to the African National Congress campaigns, but it still persisted in some cases in Mufulira. When taxed about rudeness to African customers, the Chamber admitted that many of its junior assistants were rude, but, somewhat naïvely, added that they were rude to Europeans as well. And so the list of grievances piled up, and the D.C. in cross-examination admitted that all of them were legitimate and called for a remedy.

The magistrate, in passing judgment, acquitted all the accused and declared that he had no hesitation in saying that the boycotters had sufficient justification for their action. There was no evidence, he said, that the boycott had been organized to force recognition of the Congress. The evidence showed that its object was to redress the grievances of the African consumer.

A crowd of about 300 Africans gave an ovation to the Congress President Mr H. Nkumbula and the four accused when they came out of the court room, and there can be no doubt that the successful outcome of the trial gave an enormous boost to Congress throughout the entire African population of Northern Rhodesia. So much is this the case that it can seriously be doubted whether the law department of Northern Rhodesia was wise in instituting the prosecution. It knew, or could have known had it made due enquiry, that the grievances of the African consumer population were undeniable and weighty, and it should have known therefore that the prospects of securing a conviction were slight. Immense pressure may have been brought to bear upon it by the trading bodies concerned, but it should have had the strength and wisdom to resist this pressure.

This case showed up in a high light the dangerous dualism of control which exists at the present moment in Northern Rhodesia. There is the Federal government which professes to follow a policy of racial partnership. There is the territorial government, under which comes the department of justice, which must bear the responsibility in a large manner for the state of affairs revealed by the Mufulira case, and which, apparently, is responsible for the attitude of the Chambers of Commerce in refusing to recognize or meet Congress.

The primary objective of Congress is to improve the lot of the up-to-now badly exploited African, either by negotiation, or by action, where negotiation fails. In this way, the gap between the privileged and the underdog is being narrowed; and the narrower the gap, the greater chance there is of the different races living together in peace and harmony.

The African is more sure today of what he is doing than he has ever been. This confidence in himself is mounting every day so people would do well to co-operate with him. Any student of history will recognize and understand it. It was there in India, in Burma, in Ghana, and in many other countries. Where it was handled properly it brought peace and harmony between men of colour and where it was not, it brought disaster for everybody. Our situation today demands statesmanship of the first order.

Northern Rhodesia is a country of deep-rooted contrasts, deep-rooted because everything has been planned on *apartheid* lines, everything has been running, is running and within the foreseeable future will continue to run, on those lines. In this lies the root of all the present trouble. This 'apartheid' of political, economic and social planning is admittedly more pronounced here because it takes racial lines and so must be faced as such. It is difficult for one who is genuinely interested in making multi-racialism successful to think of those at the helm of the governments concerned as being serious-minded about the racial problem.

It is useless merely to express pious hopes, or to persist in calling us agitators and self-seekers. Shall we be up to the mark and draw practical examples of what has been taking place in other countries recently? In Kenya, Kenyatta and his assistants who were called names were removed and punished, result – there was no responsible African national- ist leader to negotiate with, and the terrible and sad suffer- ing that has befallen Kenya resulted. In Uganda, the Kabaka was removed as a possible agitator and trouble-maker with the sad results we all know. In Cyprus, Archbishop Makarios and his friends were removed in the firm hope that once they were taken away all would be well. When we draw these examples let it not be thought that we are planning violence. These are facts which must be examined very carefully. We put them forward in the firm belief that we may profit as a country from the sad history of our friends.

Now, what do these so-called African malcontents, agita- tors and self-styled leaders do? Who are these people who go to prison, or suffer detention, even after courts have found them innocent? Who are these people who sacrifice comfort for bullets? Is there any personal gain or joy in knowing that these terrible things await one? In all sincerity there is none. Yet these people go out and tell their own folk that they are not paid enough, they live in slums, they have had bad schools, bad hospitals; they are discriminated against in all public places because they are not represented in councils that plan their destinies, and all this because they happen to be black. They tell them that unless they can organize themselves in the same way as white men are they will for ever remain where they are. Africans see that they are only attended to after organizing themselves and taking positive action. After promised reforms, after Royal Com- missions have gone into the issues concerned, the findings and recommendations are set aside simply because settlers shout against them. African leaders are blamed by their own followers for having negotiated with those in power who fail to keep their word. The people in power are destroying all future chances for negotiation.

We now come to the second part of the question, 'Why do they go about organizing their people in the way they do?' The answer to this is short and simple. They do so for exactly the same reasons as white politicians and trade unionists, to safeguard the interests of their people.

The third question and obviously the most important in the circumstances is, 'What should be done?' In the past, we have told those concerned that the answer lay in removing African grievances in the industrial, social and political spheres and we feel it is a sheer waste of time to say anything more.

12

Visit to the United Kingdom

I shall always remember the year 1957. It was then that I visited the United Kingdom for the first time. I was invited by the Labour party to attend a socialist conference. Mr Nkumbula and I left Northern Rhodesia for Britain on 26 May, and arrived in London the following day. We spent the early part of our visit at the Commonwealth Conference organized by the Labour party at the Beatrice Webb House in Dorking, Surrey. This conference was attended by delegates from 26 countries. They came from independent states like Australia, Canada, New Zealand, and Ghana; others came from semi-independent states like Nigeria, and the rest from countries still under foreign control like Northern Rhodesia. Generally speaking, all delegates were, to varying degrees, believers in socialist ideals.

We used our spare time interesting prominent delegates like Dr Evatt, Leader of the Opposition in the Australian Parliament (Labour party), in our problems, and the discussion usually resulted in serious condemnation of the Central African Federation.

After the conference, we busied ourselves addressing M.P.s and various interested groups of people in our problems. We sought an appointment with the Colonial Secretary, but the Kenya constitutional crisis interfered with our arrangements and before we could meet the Colonial Secretary Mr Nkumbula had to return home leaving me to continue with the work.

As both the co-operative movement and local government study needed more time than I was allowed, I decided to do a short study of British political institutions with emphasis on 'Party Organization'. I chose to examine the organization of the British Labour party with a view to ascertaining what lessons, if any, could be drawn for the improved working of the African National Congress of Northern Rhodesia. It must be remembered, however, that the Labour party was then over 50 years old; it works in a community where educational standards are high, where an exceptionally high level of political tolerance has been achieved and where the population is, for the sake of this argument, homogeneous. Above all, the Labour party is subject to no disabilities in law which are not incumbent upon any other political parties, and a universal adult franchise operates in an atmosphere where freedom of speech, writing and association are accepted as part of the natural order of the universe. A far cry from Northern Rhodesia!

I went ahead, making our problems known. I addressed meetings, large and small, in different cities and towns. I spoke to M.P.s, mainly Labour, trade unionists, clergymen, professors, press men and many other influential groups of people. Great interest and sympathy was shown. Their common request was, 'Please keep us well posted and we will do what we can to help you.' On the whole, I found the British public becoming more and more concerned with our problems and I recommended to Congress on my return the idea of having our own, well-informed representative in Britain during the next three years. It was important that we should do so. The Federal government at Rhodesia House was using very intensive propaganda to hoodwink the British public into believing that the economic case they were giving wide publicity to, was advantageous to all inhabitants of the Federation. They painted us as extremists who had no regard for human values and whose sole interest was to gain political power so we could drive white people into the sea. Cheap as these tactics were, they succeeded in causing a great deal of fear in certain influential circles.

I found that six months was not long enough to get to understand thoroughly the intricate system of British political institutions. However, I found the study of 'How the Labour party works' very fascinating. With the help of the party's Commonwealth section under John Hatch, I attended some of their summer and week-end schools. I also visited a number of local parties to see the practical side of things.

I was not able to enjoy my stay in Britain as much as I should have done, because I always carried with me the burden of the struggle going on at home. The people whom I met in England who were interested in Africa were very kind and polite and sympathetic, but like my European liberal friends in Rhodesia, they were political babes in the wood. They would never really believe what I said about the oppression of my people in the rural areas. While they were dismissing me as a gentle extremist, I was getting letters from our organizers in the Northern and Eastern Provinces which deeply wounded me. They told of continuing injustice, and of all kinds of oppression.

When I am asked by Europeans how the situation got out of hand in 1961, I try to explain something of the long history of oppression in the Northern Province, but I can see they often do not believe that I am speaking the truth. I was so worried in August 1957 by what was happening that I wrote and asked Mr Lennox-Boyd, Secretary of State for the Colonies, for an interview. I was told that I might see Lord Perth, and we did in fact meet. But I found him quite unsympathetic. He began to lecture me about the need for patience, and I am afraid we parted company not on the best of terms, and having achieved nothing.

During all my time in Britain, Titus Mukopo, the Congress Acting Secretary, kept me well informed of what was happening at home. He told me of the formation of the Constitution party, a party composed of sincere and well-meaning Europeans who, apart from the veteran politician, Dr Scott, were just playing at the political game. It was in this party that Colin Morris and Merfyn Temple first began to spread their wings. They have flown a long way since those days. The Constitution party never, of course, came within a thousand miles of challenging the African National Congress, and it began to break up at its first congress in February 1958, only four months after its formation, when it decided not to oppose Federation.

I wrote and told Titus that the time for an opposition party had not yet come. 'Once we have the vote, then one does not care how many blinking parties are formed. Some of us will have done our duty, and hope to settle down to peaceful farming. But until then, we must guard very jealously what has been achieved in the way of national unity.'

While I was in England, I was granted a scholarship to study at New Delhi University, and was greatly looking forward to taking this up, but the situation in Congress had become critical. It was reported that the constitution was to be changed to give more power to the president, and that the 'non-violence' clause might be revised.

In response to a telegram from Mr Nkumbula, I flew home arriving just as the Annual Congress was meeting in Lusaka. Unfortunately, the press attempted to build me up as a rival to Mr Nkumbula and this aroused suspicions which I had the greatest difficulty in allaying. I was determined at that time that Congress must present a united front to the world in its fight against oppression.

At the beginning of February 1958, for the first time since Congress's formation ten years previously, the Governor of Northern Rhodesia, Sir Arthur Benson, agreed to meet our representatives to discuss the proposed new Constitution for the Territory. We prepared our proposals, and in the document presented by Mr Nkumbula and myself we emphasized the need for drastic change:

Congress has, for a period of seven years now, put forward proposals for Government consideration and such proposals have found their way to the waste paper baskets. Indeed, as a result of this, an attitude of resentment and frustration among African leaders and their followers has been created. The thing is, we must repeat it, to work out a scheme which will provide an antidote for the prevailing racial bitterness and hatred.

The crux of the matter lay in our franchise proposals and in the warning with which we ended:

The franchise proposals shall be based on the acceptance of universal adult franchise of ONE MAN ONE VOTE. We have made ourselves abundantly clear in the previous paragraphs that there shall be no need for a qualitative franchise apart from age and sanity since reserved seats for the minority groups shall be created which will remove the danger of the minority groups being swamped by Africans. This is Congress's proposal, and Congress's proposal is the proposal of the Africans of the Protectorate of Northern Rhodesia.

Furthermore, we wish to give this warning to the authorities that if it is the desire of the British Government in the United Kingdom and the European settlers in Central Africa to build a healthy plural society in this part of the world, this is the time to do it. Proposals similar to the Federal franchise and the attempts which are being made to thwart a healthy political advancement of the Africans by technicalities of a qualified franchise constitute a serious threat to such a society. A qualified franchise now being proposed will leave hundreds of thousands of Africans without a vote. Naturally, these will organize propaganda campaigns against the privileged few which will create an atmosphere of unrest in the Protectorate –

an atmosphere which is bound to embarrass the Government of the day and plant fear in the minds of the minorities. In such a situation, it is idle and absolutely mischievous to talk about building a healthy and sound multi-racial society.

No wonder the country was in turmoil. 'Paramountcy of native interest' was the political guide line of the British Protectorate up to 1949. This was interpreted to mean '. . . if and when the interests of the indigenous people conflict with those of immigrant races, those of the former shall prevail' (Devonshire Declaration, 1923). This has always been too much of a stumbling block for settlers whose unyielding ambition has been amalgamation of the two Rhodesias to which Africans on the other hand are vehemently opposed. In 1948, this policy was replaced by the so-called 'Partnership' without any respect for African opinion. Later, we were told it was the foundation stone of the new Federal State of Northern Rhodesia, Southern Rhodesia and Nyasaland.

Lord Malvern, Welensky's co-architect of the Federation had, just like his friend, never hidden his contempt for Africans. As the Federation's first prime minister, he spoke of this partnership thus, '. . . it is the same as exists between rider and horse.' The settler is the rider and the African is the horse. In March of 1958, he was to tell the House of Lords, 'Africans are all liars until they are very much advanced.' (*Northern News,* 26 March 1958.)

It was to these prophets of *apartheid* posing as believers in partnership that the British Government sold us when they imposed Federation in 1953. It was small wonder, therefore, that we found twentieth-century democracy in Northern Rhodesia on all fours with the undeveloped democracy of

Ancient Greece which was enjoyed by free men and warriors while barring peasants, slaves and foreigners. When people such as these are at the helm, they make high-sounding declarations that hoodwink the world into believing they are liberals and yet they work constitutions that, in effect, place all political power in their own hands.

I must confess that as Mr Nkumbula and I were walking together up the steps of Government House – it was the first time I had ever crossed its portals – I thought our proposals were so moderate that the Government would find it difficult to dismiss them. It did not take me long to discover how wrong I was. The British lion, aged and toothless as it now is, was not a beast to be approached moderately unless you meant to sell your people to it. I remember Governor Benson asking me, 'Mr Kaunda, don't you think Europeans would paralyse Government if we accepted your proposals?' In reply I said, 'Are you implying, Your Excellency, that for our demands to be met we have got to be in a position to paralyse Government?' My question was never answered.

When the Government's proposals were announced, we were deeply shocked. Mr Nkumbula publicly burnt the White Paper in which they were contained. The franchise provided nothing more than the existing Federal franchise, plus some even more reactionary measures. Of the eight African seats, six were to be elected on the special (lower) roll and were in the rural areas. Any candidate contesting these rural seats had to get two-thirds of the Chiefs in his constituency to sign the certificate approving his candidature. Further, each of these Chiefs had to approve of the candidature in the presence of a representative of the Crown duly appointed by the Governor. We all knew that the Chiefs were in the pocket of the Administration.

One of the greatest weaknesses of this constitution was that, in practice, it was not possible for an African to contest and win any of the fourteen European seats because only a handful of Africans had qualified for the 'ordinary voters roll' while on the other hand European parties found stooges among Africans to stand on their party tickets.

When the election was held in two of the special seats, the candidates had not been able to get the necessary certificates from the Chiefs. Two Africans got in on Welensky's Federal party ticket with votes from Europeans. Sir John Moffat's Central African party obtained two seats, the Congress one, and there was one independent African from Barotseland.

Once more, we were told that our fears were groundless when, in fact, political chicanery had been the order of the day. It was not long before Welensky was asking that the Federation should be declared a Republic.

13

I Split With Harry Nkumbula

The African National Congress has always stated its belief in non-violence and, as the years went by, I became more and more convinced that the only way is to win your enemies to your way of thinking and not to defeat them by violence.

In a letter to James Johnson of the Labour party written on 30 July 1957, I said:

'I have been in the field now for just over six years. The rate at which my people are becoming politically awake is frightening, and already we are seeing a situation arising whereby our present Congress Executive could be replaced by a more radical one, which might think our present methods of non-violence, a not fast enough method of re-dressing our grievances. I know now, James, that it is not the leaders that have been responsible for violent activities in colonial countries. I have never in the past thought of any African calling the present Executive of the African National Congress a compromising and dangerously moderate Council, but this is already happening and all I am asking the British Government is to help us to settle these matters peacefully by telling them the danger of growing African opposition to these in democratic set-ups. I would be the last person to advocate violence because apart from the fact that it does not pay, we have only our people to get killed. What is the point in having the people one struggles for killed? Who is going to profit by those rights once they are achieved with half the population gone? In spite of the truth in my statement, I would be doing a disservice if I did not tell the British public what dangers lie ahead. I repeat what I have said for the sake of emphasis. We have no intention of running MAU MAU in our country but there are those dangers. I have pointed out those facts which I think it important for the British Government to know.'

During the early part of 1958, I suffered a good deal from illness and the doctors could not seem to get to the bottom of it. I had one terrible journey from the Eastern Province when my lungs became full of dust. At that time, I was very grateful for all the help I received from the Salvation Army doctor at Chikankata, Dr S. G. Gauntlett. Not only did he do much in helping my recovery to good health but on his busy rounds of the wards, he would stop at my bedside for long and interesting discussions. I am glad to count him still among my friends.

During this time, my interest in 'non-violence' policies was quickened. In my Congress Circular of 31 January 1958, I wrote:

It is a good coincidence that we should be writing on this very important subject at the time when not only India but the entire world is remembering the Father of India and the man who put the powerful weapon of 'non-violence' into practice. With it, he defied one of the then most powerful imperial and world powers – the British Empire. For years, he brought suffering upon his own body and ended up a victim of a dirty tool of imperialism. We might add this that it was perhaps fitting that he should end up like that . . . a more noble end could not be found.

For the last seven years, our national leader and President has stressed the need for being non-violent in our struggle. This has worked out wonderfully well. Africans have behaved remarkably well even in the face of provocation. But let us say there is a limit to everything. Last year's annual conference of the African National Congress saw leaders hard put to defending this principle. Most delegates were in favour of removing the clause that deals with this from our constitution. Only the trust and confidence the rank and file have placed in their leaders saved the clause. What does this mean? Some people will argue that if violence broke out in Northern Rhodesia it is only the Africans who would suffer. Nobody knows this better

With Lewis Changufu touring in the Northern Province after the 'troubles'

UNO 1962 – Shaking hands with Mr Chandra S. Jha, Chairman of the General Assembly's Special Committee of 17

'Bingo!', a cartoon by Vicky published in the Evening Standard

than Congress leaders. We are aware that violence would invite South African troops, British troops, American troops too might come in if, for instance, what has been happening in Algeria and Cyprus happens here. Congress leaders realize, therefore, that they have a moral duty to keep their people away from imperial bullets.

We put in this article in an effort to try and persuade Government to stop what it is doing now. . . . We have evidence to show how provocative Government or its agents have been. The police mobile unit's activities in the Northern and Luapula Provinces leaves much to be desired of any police force in a democratic country. Boma messengers have done untold harm to relations between Africans and Government; have they behaved so badly without instructions from their white superiors? In a most recent case, a District Commissioner actually went down to a Congress committee meeting and ordered the police mobile unit to beat up Congress men, women and children who were very orderly. What is Government up to? Shall we conclude that the police and military forces that are being built are there to turn Northern Rhodesia into a police state as far as Africans are concerned?

We implore all our officers everywhere to stress more and more to all our people to remain non-violent. We must deny Government a chance for mowing our people down with machine-guns. It has happened before on the Copperbelt and it can happen on a larger scale if we give them a chance. This does not mean that you should co-operate with what is evil, far from it. Refuse to have anything to do with anything that is unworthy of man.

In May 1958, I was invited by the Indian Council for Cultural Relations to visit India. I had been disappointed that I had been unable to go to New Delhi so I welcomed this opportunity of visiting Gandhi's homeland to meet many of those who had taken part in those non-violent demonstrations which had helped to win India her independence. It was a wonderful experience for which I shall always be grateful but it was only an interlude in our own long struggle, so has little place here.

I now turn to a less happy theme. Anyone who had known my relations with Mr Nkumbula during the years we worked together, first as District Secretary for Chinsali (1951-52), then as his Provincial Organizing Secretary for the Northern Province (1952-53) and finally as his Secretary-General (1953-58), would be justified in expressing surprise at what appeared to be a sudden parting. The parting was sad but inevitable at the time it took place.

We all knew and appreciated how much Mr Nkumbula had done ever since he took over from Mr Mbikusita. But I take the view that it would have been national suicide politically to have allowed Mr Nkumbula to continue to guide the nation in the way he was doing. Some of our critics are quick to point out to us that we should have removed him from the Presidency instead of ourselves breaking away. I hope those will be wiser when they have realized what was happening inside Congress at that time. I will here point out our reasons for breaking away, without harming my old friend's reputation in any way.

For all the time we were together, the A.N.C. constitution provided that the top officials of the Congress, namely, President, Secretary, Treasurer and their deputies shall all be elected after three years in office at an appropriate conference. But when Mr Nkumbula realized that he had made himself unpopular, he started planning to change the Congress constitution so that its President could be elected on the same pattern as that of the United States of America by setting up polling booths at every branch. This, he thought, would make him some sort of life President of Congress as he would depend on his past popularity in so far as branch members were concerned. All of us at the top with him refused to accept such an unnecessarily costly affair which, above all, would lead us to nepotism and despotism within Congress, the very evils we are fighting against outside.

Mr Nkumbula began to brand anyone who opposed anything he wanted as either a Communist or a sell-out. No matter how wise one may be, one is bound to make mistakes, and if in any party or any group of people members fear to criticize their leader constructively for fear of being branded either Communists or sell-outs, then it all becomes a one-man show and you are right on the verge of dictatorship. This is where we were in Congress at that time.

At the April 1957 meeting of the National Executive Council, we agreed to send a delegation to Britain of the top three officials (this was cut to two due to lack of funds). We also agreed to support the delegation with boycotts of beer halls. This beer hall boycott was also to support our demand that beer-brewing should be taken over by co-operative societies run by Africans. At that time, all the municipal councils and management boards which ran these beer halls had no African representation at all so that when the thousands of pounds that came from Africans were expended, the African people had no say at all. This was the position when Mr Nkumbula and I flew to London. Two days before we were due to meet the Colonial Secretary, Mr Nkumbula decided to fly back home. I tried to argue with him about the necessity of his meeting Mr Lennox-Boyd but he replied by asking me whether I was afraid of meeting him alone. I told him it was not a matter of being afraid but that I was only the humble Secretary-General. He was the President now in Britain with an appointment already made with the Colonial Secretary. It was important for him to hold on only for two more days and then he could leave. But he decided to go back home, and he did. The result was that we did not see the Colonial Secretary and I was told to see Lord Perth, Minister of State for the Colonies.

There was another engagement for Mr Nkumbula. He was supposed to go to Ireland after meeting the Colonial Secretary but he went away and it was my shameful duty to defend my President by fabricating stories of why he had to depart so suddenly, and I hope the people concerned will forgive me when they read through these lines.

When Mr Nkumbula came back home he would not deal with Mr Kapwepwe, the very man he had left in his position but went ahead to call off the boycotts which his own National Executive Council had called. It was a sad thing, but it happened. The result was our provincial colleagues suffered because those in authority in government could point to the leader of the party denouncing his own boycotts and they accused his subordinates of calling boycotts without his consent.

One of the most fatal mistakes that Mr Nkumbula made was to fall into the habit of inviting Mr Harry Franklin to our sessions of the National Executive Council whenever he thought there was an issue that might raise serious controversies. What he did not appreciate at this point when he was gradually feeling he was losing his popularity is the fact that members of his Executive respected him more than they did Harry Franklin. We simply could not treat Congress at this time of our development as if we were an African Welfare Association with ex-D.C. 'Bwana' Franklin coming

94

to call us all sorts of names. The very last of these invitations was related to the question of the beer-hall boycotts referred to above. Mr Franklin had the cheek to call members of the National Executive Council 'barbarians' because of these boycotts. As could be expected, some members walked out of this Council. What Mr Nkumbula thought he would gain by this friendship only he can say. One thing, however, stood clear, and that is, all progressive elements in that National Executive Council who had faith in Mr Nkumbula began to lose it. Were these insults to the Council an arranged affair between the two Harrys or was it done on the spur of the moment? Only they can tell us.

Even after these incidents, I tried to maintain faith in the man I had always called 'the Old Man' as a mark of respect until I came back from Britain on his instructions. I had cut my course short as I was going to India but on hearing that there was trouble in the Congress and he, my President, wanted me back, I came back. When I arrived, Frank Barton, an expert journalist, reproduced in the *African Times* an article he had first written in the *Central African Post* under the title, HE GOES TO CHURCH EVERY SUNDAY AND PLANS TWENTY YEARS HENCE. The title he gave his article this time was, KAUNDA, THE MAN TO WATCH. This caused a lot of trouble in Mr Nkumbula's mind. He spoke to me seriously about this article and told me that this was not helping me at all. I told him that I had nothing to do with the *African Times'* article. He said if that was the case, I should refute it. When I gladly did this, his anxiety rested for a while.

During my tour of India which I took after the World Assembly of Youth conference in Dar-es-Salaam, Mr Nkumbula went round suspending and expelling all those provincial officials that he believed had lost confidence in him. He suspended the majority of officers in the Luapula, Eastern, Northern and Western Provinces. The result was that the only two – Northern and Central – which he did not suspend, passed a vote of no confidence in him.

During my absence, Congress borrowed some money and sent Mr Nkumbula to London, together with a government official delegation which included Mr Sokota and Mr Chileshe. To begin with, the Colonial Office refused to meet Mr Nkumbula but the two African members of the Legislative Council mentioned above managed to persuade Governor Benson to allow Mr Nkumbula to meet the Colonial Secretary. When his time came for this appointment, he was still resting in bed at his hotel – why? Only he can tell us. The only thing he could do was to post his memorandum to the Colonial Office. Was this the way to represent the African National Congress?

Those of us who have followed the trend of political events closely know that Mr Nkumbula burnt the White Paper on the Federation of Rhodesia and Nyasaland. He would have nothing to do with it until he allowed Mr Francis Chembe, a member of the Federal Parliament, to join Congress without first of all resigning from the Federal Parliament. This, together with the time of the Federal elections when the late Mr Lawrence Katilungu was allowed by Mr Nkumbula to do some electioneering at a Congress conference after the split in October 1958, are the only two times that Mr Nkumbula has been anywhere near Federation. Even if we excuse both as purely accidental, when it came to the territorial constitution, Mr Nkumbula's behaviour left much to be desired.

Even before the National Executive Council discussed this proposed constitution, Mr Nkumbula was busy flirting with the Constitution party. We were in fact waiting for him to come and open an important session of the Executive when he was going round pact-making. When he did finally arrive, it was to try and persuade us that we could form a coalition government by winning the eight seats for Africans and then joining hands with the Constitution party which he said was certain of winning eight of the European seats. We dismissed this as political prostitution at best and a complete sell-out at worst. We cross-examined our leader on various points of the proposed constitution and he who came boasting that he had mastered it, in actual fact, left us with the impression he had not begun to understand it. The result was we set up a sub-committee of six members to reply to the White Paper. The six were Reuben C. Kamanga, Solomon Kalulu, Simon Kapwepwe, Justin Chimba, Titus B. Mukupo and myself. The reply gave our reasons for rejecting the Benson Constitution and is contained in Appendix III.

Shortly after our findings, Mr Nkumbula burnt in public a copy of the White Paper on the constitution of Northern Rhodesia and we took it for granted that he, as our leader, had put a seal to this bogus constitution fraught with political snares and pitfalls. As already pointed out above, he had done something similar over the White Paper on Federation. It was a complete surprise to some of us, therefore, to see our leader wanting to give this very constitution a 'fair trial'. This was the final straw.

Not unnaturally, we began to ask ourselves a number of questions, some of which were, Was this the man who had inspired us at the time of fighting against Federation, the man who had inspired us by renaming the Northern Rhodesia African Congress, 'The African National Congress'? Was he now asking for powers he had never found necessary ever since he took over from Mr Mbikusita? We went on, Is the man we have trusted now demanding something he knows is wrong even before he has that power constitutionally? Is he not packing the National Executive Council with non-members, men and women who were not even provincial officers? I wondered whether this was still the same man, the man to whom I had given my unqualified support and loyalty, the man I had known to be unyielding to anything because of his love for his people and country. I wondered why he was behaving like this. Mr Nkumbula was a man who because of his nationalism could not even allow anything tribalistic to be discussed in his National Executive Council but who was now busy trying to split us all on tribal lines. It was terrible and incredible but there was no point in deceiving ourselves for sad as all this was, it was happening. I began wondering whether he was becoming a second Mbikusita. The question now is, What made Mr Nkumbula change his behaviour like that? No other person can answer this except himself. Others can only guess. If he won't answer, history will. For while we can cheat and fool one another, we cannot do the same with history. Let us only hope that history will not judge him too harshly, for he was sincere in his early days.

We left the African National Congress without anything. All we had was a tide of anger against us. On 24 October, the Zambia African Congress was born at a meeting held at Broken Hill to which sixty delegates had been called with only a week's notice. I was elected President, Mr Sipalo the Secretary and Mr Kapwepwe the Treasurer. Mr D. Konkola, Mr W. K. Sikalumbi and Mr R. C. Kamanga were elected as our deputies, but as soon as Mr Konkola discovered that he had not been chosen as President, he walked out of the meeting and Mr Paul Kalichini was elected a deputy in his place. As soon as the elections were over, we set about our task and we really worked hard. Today when we meet and recall our system of organization and the spirit behind it all, we are staggered by the amount of work we managed to get through.

Our headquarters was hut number 280 at the New Chilenje township. We had to live there as well as use it for our office. We drew up a scheme of work for each day and also we kept a careful record of all work done. This scheme of work was a sheet of paper headed, 'Where is it?' Each one of us had to go out every night of the week to a location, compound or section of a township as had been assigned to us on the list. We had just three points to deal with. The first was to tell people why we had broken with the African National Congress; the second was to explain in detail why we had rejected the Benson constitution for the territory. The third was an appeal for membership and subscriptions.

Every morning we met to report on the previous night's successes and failures and then we would draw up the new scheme of work for the day.

Where there had been success, we knew that there was less need for concentration, except to check on the appointed organizers from time to time. Even if we were out of the headquarters, there would always be someone junior to receive reports and report back to us. Our slogans became very popular. We invented and introduced easy slogans so that all our followers could repeat them, for the more people you had shouting them the better for the popularity and membership campaign of the party. Within a few weeks, we grew to something very considerable.

I should like to point out here that reading the Ridley Report today I can see that those who were informing Governor Benson about our activities at night could have taken our seriousness in organizing our people at night as intimidating and threatening them. This was not true. When the Ridley Report speaks of violence being planned to take place after we were arrested for violent speeches, I believe all that to be some sort of excuse to suit the action taken by Government then. It must be common sense to any unbiased observer that the moment you remove leaders from their followers, each one of those followers becomes a general unto himself. There are numerous examples in the Indian struggle for independence. Whenever leaders were arrested violence broke out almost invariably. In fact, for all the allegations in the press, radio and through various other media, we never planned violence of any kind. The only charge ever made against me for my activities at this time was that I had conspired with others to call an unauthorized meeting. This, of course, is regarded as a felony and when it was reported in the press that I was charged with conspiring to commit a felony, it appeared to the casual reader that I was planning something horrible. In a later chapter, I state that this calling of an unauthorized meeting was done in accordance with a procedure we had clearly laid down to give due warning to Government if we planned in any way to break the law. I had in actual fact raised the question with Governor Benson by petitioning him three times for permission to hold meetings and when he refused to allow us any more meetings, I felt it was my duty to defend freedom of speech by defying what we all regarded as a stupid ban.

While we were busy day and night organizing our new party, we found time to draw up our own proposals for constitutional reform which we submitted to the British government on 4 February 1959. Printed on the front of our proposals was the text: 'We know of no other repository of the ultimate powers of society but the people themselves.'

In our letter to the Colonial Secretary we said, 'Government is the strongest of which every man feels himself a part', and this, of course, was the fundamental basis of our demand for a universal franchise. It is the possession of the vote that makes a man or woman feel in himself that he is a real part of the new nation.

The document we presented is too long to quote here in full; but it is interesting to note that the proposals we made in our Zambia days when everyone was calling us thugs and hooligans were not very different from the constitution given us by the British government in 1962. I quote the relevant paragraphs under Articles 2, 3 and 4 of our proposals:

Article 2. Franchise

1 Every male or female African on or above the age of 20 years shall have the right to vote;

2 Alien Africans on or above the age of 20 years shall have the right to vote after six months' residence;

3 Alien Non-Africans on or above the age of 21 years after 3 years' residence and being an approved citizen, shall have the right to vote.

4 Alien Non-Africans from Britain and other Western democracies on or above the age of 21 years shall have the vote immediately on naturalization or otherwise after 3 years' residence;

5 Non-Africans from South African and other imperial

possessions in Africa on or above the age of 25 years shall have the vote immediately after naturalization or after 5 years of residence.

Article 3. Representation

There shall be a Parliament of 59 members directly elected by the people plus *three* ex-officio members – Chief Secretary, Attorney-General and Financial Secretary.

1 The 59 shall be elected thus: two elected members for each of the following towns (eight of whom shall be non-Africans): Livingstone, Lusaka, Broken Hill, Ndola, Luanshya, Mufulira, Kitwe – Kalulushi – Chilubuma, Chingola – Bancroft.

2 Four elected members from the four farming areas of the Southern, Eastern, Central and Western Provinces.

3 39 shall be elected thus: Barotseland, 5; N.W. Province, 4; Western Province (Rural), 3; Luapula Province, 4; Northern Province, 7; Eastern Province, 6; Southern Province, 4; Central Province, 6; making 39 in all.

The National Council of Chiefs

There shall be a Central Council of Chiefs. All Paramount Chiefs shall be ex-officio Members of the National Council of Chiefs. All Native Authorities shall return one.

Meetings

The National Council of Chiefs shall meet four times a year.

Powers of the National Council of Chiefs

(a) Shall safeguard customary law, culture and traditions.

(b) Shall act as guardians and custodians of the Nation by:
  (i) Checking on legislations that affect the Nation as in (a) above.
  (ii) Checking on any other legislation.

Article 4. The Parliament

There shall be a House of representatives hereinafter known as the 'National Assembly'. The National Assembly shall be presided over by a Speaker elected by the National Assembly.

With the exception of Ministries of Defence, Foreign Affairs, Finance and Law which shall be held by the Governor, and three top Civil Servants, the Cabinet shall consist of nine Ministries nominated by the leader of the majority Party from among the elected members in consultation with the Governor. These shall be the Chief Minister (Home Affairs and National Guidance) and the Ministries for Commerce and Industry, Economic Planning and Mineral Wealth; Agriculture and Natural Resources; Land Development and Co-operatives; Labour; Health; Education; Information and Broadcasting; Local Government; Transport and Communication. The Ministers shall owe allegiance to the British Crown. There shall be permanent Under Secretaries to all the Ministries appointed at the discretion of the responsible Ministers. The Under Secretaries shall not sit in the National Assembly.

14

Arrest and Detention

The day had been unsually hot for March and the out-of-
season drought made the little ones who lay uncomfortably
sprawled on their communal mats rather tired. In a two-
roomed house, number 257, New Chilenje township, ten
of us lived. There were two nieces and a nephew besides my
wife and our five sons. Our nephew and our firstborn shared
our small kitchen. There they lay, looking more like pieces of
firewood than human beings. The youngest two shared our
tiny bedroom with us and the rest occupied the other room.
It was everything – bedroom, living-room, dining-room – and
before we secured a New Chilenje two-roomed house number
280, this room was also used as the Zambia office. In fact, it
was here that the resolution to form the Zambia African
National Congress was passed. The congestion and the dis-
comfort I knew to be too hard on my wife who was expecting
our sixth child, but she did not complain. This suffering has,
however, now been a source of great laughter between the
Kapwepwes and ourselves for, in their own moments, Mama
Salome Kapwepwe and my wife very seriously questioned
the wisdom of their husbands starting a new political party.
Had we not suffered enough when serving in the African
National Congress and was it not time we went back to a
normal life, the life we had known in pre-Congress
activities? However, this was carefully hidden from us.

On 10 March, one of our informants came to report that all senior police officers from all Provinces had been meeting at their territorial Headquarters and he knew we were going to be arrested, either on that day or the following. We, therefore, began to prepare ourselves by combing our offices and homes clean in so far as our valued papers and books were concerned. We placed these with people we could trust and those we knew the police could not suspect and invade. By this time we had already sent out to Tanganyika Mr Lewis Changufu. We did not have sufficient funds but Mr Ben Kapufi, then a business man in Broken Hill, offered to assist us. The original idea was that both Mr Munukayumbwa Sipalo and Mr Reuben Chitandika Kamanga, National Secretary and Deputy National Treasurer respectively, would leave the Protectorate, but lack of funds prevented this.

On 10 March nothing unusual happened. On the 11th, it was clear that we were being shadowed in a very unusual way and we knew the reason for it. Late that evening about five of us got together. It is now difficult to say why we met. Perhaps our souls and bodies needed coming together. However, we were together for some good hours until someone joked it would be better that one should be arrested in the presence of his own family, and that sent us all to our respective homes. All of us had heavy hearts even though each tried hard not to display it. By the time I got home all but my wife were fast asleep. I could not find our lock so I used a pair of scissors in place of a lock.

I must have been asleep for an hour when I opened my eyes and noticed that a motor vehicle was approaching our home and had floodlit our bedroom. My watch read 1 a.m. I began to dress and told my wife to do likewise. Before we could go through there was a loud knock at our cattle-kraal-type door. In a very firm voice I said, 'Just a moment, please.' This was followed up by a big push and the pair of scissors gave way and, in the twinkling of an eye, there was a policeman in uniform right in our bedroom.

He immediately ordered me to put my signature to a piece of paper which he would neither show nor read to me. Normally, I would have refused to sign something that I knew nothing about, but this time I looked at my wife and then my two boys with their startled faces and without the slightest resistance I signed a document not knowing what it was. Up to now, I cannot explain my action. It was not as though I was taken by surprise. I knew they were coming and my mind was steady in so far as I can remember . . . so it could not be a surprise. However, he ordered that I should pack up one suitcase while his two colleagues filled their Land-Rover with my books and papers. The younger of our two nieces sat up just as I was getting out and shouted, 'Za-za-za.' And just as suddenly as she had started up she fell back and slept. The whole small Land-Rover was full of my books and papers; so much so that I perched on my own otherwise valuable property with my left hand handcuffed to an African plain-clothes man and my right to that of a white assistant inspector in uniform. My wife, who had followed us outside, was told by the policeman, who obviously was leading the operation, to report at the D.C.'s office for ration money. With this, my long journey to some unknown destination started. I was rushed to the Woodlands police station. I discovered later that the man in charge did not trust the signature I had given him and so I had to thumbprint his document. From this police station, we rushed at a terrific speed past Government House, the Secretariat, the High Court and on to King George Avenue which joined

Cairo Road. Six miles from Lusaka on the Great North Road towards Broken Hill, we swerved into a very large gravel pit where some contractor had dug out ballast for the road. I thought the whole police force was centred there for the night. There must have been some forty police vehicles around. The man in charge of our unwelcome expedition reported to his superiors about his big catch and I was immediately conscious of scores of hungry and fixed glances. My suitcase was thrown to the ground and someone opened it and began to make a thorough search of all my clothes and then threw them down carelessly. After this I was pushed into a near-by Black Maria where I found two of my colleagues, Simon Kapwepwe and old John Mumbi. A few minutes later we were joined by Chipowe who was Lusaka Chairman.

The fact that we did not know where we were going made us very uncomfortable. We tried to speak to the two police officers who were in charge at this time but they would not talk, so we decided to be unruly and started singing. They did not like it, so they threatened to separate us if we continued. We thought that would be terrible in the circumstances so we stopped, but this gave me an opportunity to talk and rather unconcernedly I said, 'I am very glad that I am going to see my mother at last.' One of the two men fell into our trap. Laughing very loudly and obviously enjoying himself he said, 'You have a hope. You are going right in the opposite direction.' Well this wasn't much but at least we knew we were not going home. Incidentally, all of us five were ex-Chinsali.

It must have been between 3 and 4 a.m. when all officers and their men left except for a car, a Land-Rover and our Black Maria. At 4 o'clock we started moving. We went round and round Lusaka for about an hour and then we shot straight for the airport where we found a full force of security men. I was called out first and two hefty police officers escorted me to a waiting 44-seater plane, the engines of which were already running and ready for immediate take-off. My hands were twisted as they took me to the aeroplane. At a quarter past five we took off for our unknown destination. Our next port was Ndola. As we descended, we could see a big police truck surrounded by Land-Rovers and we knew we were stopping to pick up some more 'trouble-makers'. Sure enough we were joined by Hyden Dingiswayo Banda, Nephas Tembo, J. K. Mulenga, R. Kapangala, Joseph L. Mulenga and Ralph Kombe from Broken Hill. I remember as we were airborne again we were offered some corned beef and biscuits. Someone told the captain (a police officer) that I did not take meat but there was nothing the poor man could do. After some time, I went along to the lavatory. An African constable followed me. I protested vigorously to the captain for this intrusion into my privacy, but our good captain could only regret and told us those were his orders so I decided to withdraw. After some two hours we landed at Balovale landing ground. I spent some few hours there and was then sent on the last lap of my long journey to my unknown destination. At six p.m., I was handed over to the D.C., Kabompo. There Frank Chitambala joined me and thirty minutes later, we arrived at our new 'home'.

In *Black Government?*, which I wrote with the Rev. Colin Morris, I said, 'We are engaged in a struggle against any form of imperialism and colonialism not because it has as its agents white men but because it has many more wrong sides than good ones.' Here is an illustration of what I mean. After our first breakfast at Kabompo, we decided to take a stroll.

To our surprise villagers ran away from us as we approached them. Men stood near trees ready to climb up should we approach them. Mothers dashed to their houses with babies in their arms. When this was repeated about three times, we thought it right to find out what was happening and, on investigation, we found out that those in authority had spread a very wicked story about us. Villagers had been told that these Zambia men were cannibals. They especially liked children since these provided tender meat. Anyone who would go to this extent of telling lies in order to maintain his position I think calls for mental treatment, but this is imperialism at work. In *Black Government?* I also said, 'It is an arrangement that will corrupt the best of men regardless of their colour, creed or religion.' I can't imagine these same people who do such things in Africa doing these things in Britain, but out here they are defending a wrong system. However, very soon we settled down and our people around soon came in good numbers to listen to the good tidings of FREEDOM. In fact, we became so effective that only a month after we had been there we received individual orders banning us from addressing any meeting at all.

Our movements were restricted to a limited area so we tried to while away our time in as useful a way as we could in the circumstances. We began our mornings with baths and breakfast after which Frank and Musonda, who joined us after two weeks, would go out to look for provisions; then they would join me at our open-air office. Some very strange things happened there. One very hot morning, I was wearing a very simple form of sandal and had no shirt on, only a vest. I had been reading very hard but at this time I stopped suddenly. My thoughts began wandering. I wondered why man could not come closer to nature and be a friend with all that we fear today. I thought to myself if only we could be like little children we might play around with deadly snakes like the puff adder. At this juncture, I looked down and saw the head of a very big snake just passing the small toe of my left foot. I cannot explain my behaviour here but I looked on calmly. My uninvited, unwelcome and deadly poisonous visitor was a black mamba about five feet long. (After Mr John Gaunt called me a black mamba, I often wondered why this particular member of 'my family' did not stop to greet me. It could be my ignorance of the Mamba language!) Some good five minutes must have elapsed when all of a sudden I jumped up and dashed into my bedroom. The swift snake must have been a mile away by then.

After lunch, we would take a rest and we would go back to our open air office again until 5 p.m. I would then take my long evening walk while Frank and Musonda would prepare our evening meals. It was during these walks that another of these strange things happened. Before this time, I used to admire much that is in nature but never before had I come so close to nature and never before had I actually fallen in love with nature. This is what I mean. Before this, I had defended quite sincerely, controlled 'Chitememe System' and 'Soil Conservation' as well as game reserves. I had done this because of my personal experience at home. Around Lubwa we had plenty of game, trees and grass. But as our gun population grew, game became less and less. Today hunters have to go to Chiefs Chibale and Lundu in the Luangwa Valley to hunt game. Trees disappeared until some method of control was resorted to. We had to work hard to save our soil at the Mission Station from erosion by making contour ridges. This was my experience before Kabompo days, but quite a new attachment to nature grasped me here. I would walk for about a mile and then come to rest at a very high place overlooking one of the most beautiful scenes in the country at that time of the year. Here the silent waters of the Kabompo River gather in one great sheet of water. On both sides of the river are huge trees, deep green in the rainy season. They seem to be jealous of one another and appear to be pointing fingers of strange accusation at each other as the wind blows them backwards and forwards. Just as this one great sheet of water makes a sharp bend at the grassy feet of this princely high ground of Kabompo Boma, the silent waters burst into noisy protest as they clash with the enduring rocks.

Here I would sit in silent meditation removed from this world. Here I seemed to be getting nearer and nearer to understanding the language of nature. I studied the various shapes of trees and this gave me great pleasure. As the quiet breeze blew from the River Kabompo the trees and the grass around seemed to dance to a strange tune which made me feel that I was in the midst of music which would never come the way of my ears. However, there I sat, while minutes ran into hours. During these periods lions, leopards, hyenas, snakes and all animals seemed to accept one name, creatures of God the Almighty, and seemed to agree that they should not hurt each other. At times, Frank Chitambala would get worried about my long absence and would come looking for me. After this experience, I decided to get myself a camera, hoping to photograph trees from various angles that pleased me and to build up an album of such shapes. At this time more than ever before I began to wrestle with the idea that trees and all growing things must have a language of their own but that God's creation that passes all men's understanding has kept this a secret, and that some day this secret will be revealed to man in the same way as so many have already been revealed. I have bought my camera since coming out of jail but the factor of time is against my Kabompo detention days' ambition. I still hope to fulfil this some time.

Our influence around Kabompo was not confined to schoolboys and villagers only. I had a habit of using a rough sort of staff as a walking stick. Within a month almost every Boma messenger was walking around with one. So did a good number of schoolboys, much to the annoyance of the officials, who started giving lectures on how not to behave. Life was not all rosy at Kabompo. I almost lost my life at one time. I had a serious attack of dysentery followed by a sharp attack of malaria and then I suffered from a series of colds and coughing attacks. In so far as my health was concerned I did much better when I was re-arrested and sentenced to prison. There are other sad memories of Kabompo. One day I went to see the District Commissioner about the insufficiency of our allowances. I arrived at the offices at 8.30 a.m. At 9.30 a.m. the Hon. William Nkanza, member of the Legislative Council for North West arrived. He waited for forty-five minutes but the D.C. could not see him. We were just told to wait. Mr Nkanza went back but I still continued to wait. At 12 noon I went past the messenger posted near the D.C.'s door to stop anyone from going in. My patience was completely exhausted. I knocked at the door very angrily and entered without his asking me in. He shouted at me to get out but I refused and instead demanded to be told why he had kept me waiting for three and a half hours. He replied that he was drafting something for me to sign. I shouted back saying surely it would have been good manners to let me know and then I would not have wasted my time.

How would he have liked it if someone else had treated him as he had treated me?

At this juncture, he lost his temper and called me names. Silently I went straight for him. He left his chair and we went round and round his table as he called for his head messenger. The head messenger came in and stood between us as we looked at each other like fighting cocks. Our newly found peace-maker was an old man for whom I had great respect and, when he pleaded with me not to do anything, I looked at my friend and saying, 'I respect the head messenger more than I do you', I left. An hour later, the D.C. came to my open-air office to make us sign certain documents. They were the orders – already referred to above – banning all three of us from addressing any meetings for three months.

One other thing I think I should refer to. Before being taken to Kabompo as a detainee, I had not visited the North Western Province at all. Because of this my knowledge of this Province as well as Barotseland was only second-hand. One of the things that struck me immediately as a universal problem for our country was drunkenness. My worry about this problem can be understood by reading part of a letter to Mr Solomon Kalulu who had just resigned from the African National Congress leadership. I wrote to him at this time:

Brother Kalulu, my short stay here has been an eye-opener. I now agree with those who say in the worst of things there is always a degree of good. As you know for good or bad I have spent much of my time in the A.N.C. offices ever since I took over the secretaryship in 1953. This has made me lose sight of the rural areas. I have gone round quickly with an eye more on the politics of the day and have rushed to the Headquarters with little understanding of the vastness of the problem. In the way we are going about it today, we will be founding our National House on sand and as Our Lord has taught, this house so built will not stand the tempests that are part and parcel of what we lightly call LIFE. In this respect, I think my being arrested and rusticated has been a blessing in disguise. I have not only discovered my mistake (or rather Himalayan Error) but have in the process just started re-discovering myself and my people. I have always believed that our moral decay was rampant only in certain areas and not in rural areas. In this, I have been mistaken greatly. I don't know whether you share my feelings on this point. The Western way of life has been so powerful that our own social, cultural and political set-up has been raped by the powerful and greedy Western civilization. To crown it all, the economic disequilibrium is such that our people, having lost their social and cultural background, are now hovering around to catch up with the outwardly superior social and cultural levels of the West. This needs a certain standard of economic strength which is absent. The result is the desire to have what they cannot have or what a foreign rule has deprived them of; and so what? Of course, moral DESTRUCTION.

Now do we who style ourselves leaders of African opinion make serious surveys of this? Do we sincerely work for self-government now? If so, who do we hope to lead to our cherished land of Canaan? A nation half-drunk, half-thinking, half-corrupted, possessing only so many other halves of what makes LIFE what it should be? In short, do we hope to make a nation out of an utterly demoralized people? Is it possible? Sometimes I fear this subject haunts me so much that I may suffer from an obsession. This is difficult to say for one on his own, so I trust you will be good as ever you have been to me and tell me plainly if, from the bottom of your heart, you think

I am over-anxious about this. In other words, if you think things are not as bad as I see them please say so and supply arguments to show the contrary is the case.

Ever since I came here, I have seen young men of my age and, what is worse, some who are much younger, give no thought whatsoever. If they have their pay-packet and can get bottles of Kachasu on Saturdays and Sundays, the only concerns of life are met. What goes on here during week-ends presents as pathetic a sight as you see in Lusaka. Honestly, how can we go on like this? The mix-ups in these drinking places is such that people end up in the Chiefs' Courts on Mondays. There is no time for serious thinking and planning. Amidst all this mess, the Northern Rhodesia government is bringing a bottle store here either next month or so. This reminds me of what one of the top men in the African Affairs Committee said once when someone was arguing against beer sales increase. He said, 'How are we going to run our local government African affairs without this?' Hollow! Honestly, if a government cannot be run without demoralizing so badly its own people, then that government is no good and it must give way to people who can.

One does not object to people drinking. It is a habit that has grown with us, I mean in us the entire mankind. But I suspect it is being used to destroy us. There are so many things that are bad in our way of life but I believe there are also many that are good. Among those that are good is the way our forefathers used to take their alcoholic stuffs. It was not only dignified but was also a place at which the old imparted wisdom to the young. In fact, it is still the way all self-respecting people under all shades of colour take their drinks even today. Why should it be different for us, the African masses? Please discuss this subject with Brother Christopher and any others whom you trust and let me know what your opinion is. I don't need to say 'your candid' opinion because I trust you cannot tell anyone what you don't believe to be right. The history of the working class in Britain greatly subscribes to my fears.

On hearing from you, I shall introduce another subject and maybe in this way we could find a way out.

When we were banned, arrested and banished to various parts of the country, Governor Benson made a terrible attack on us that was widely circulated through the press and also, of course, broadcast several times. I heard then that a commission had been set up to look into the banning of Zambia and so I decided to prepare a statement to be presented to this Commission. It was to be a sworn statement. This was not presented to the Ridley Commission because my legal advisers counselled against it. The following is part of my statement:

Sworn memorandum drawn up by Kenneth David Kaunda, thirty-five-year-old ex-leader and President of the Zambia African National Congress, Northern Rhodesia, for the Commission appointed to probe into the banning of the said Zambia African National Congress, Northern Rhodesia.

To begin with, I wish the Commissioner to know that I am disadvantageously placed when drawing up this memorandum in that documents from which I could have drawn specific references to support my case are all in the custody of the Northern Rhodesia police, and that all persons that I could have asked to come forward as witnesses are similarly placed. In the circumstances, I can do no better than base my memorandum on the Governor's statement as reported in the *Central African Post* of 13 March 1959.

The Governor has taken the drastic step of not only

banning a four-month-old popular African political
organization but has also arrested and rusticated all its
leaders without trial in courts of law. It is astounding
that he has given such a weak case to explain why he took
this step. I will here give evidence to show the Commission
that there was either colossal ignorance of the truth on
certain important matters upon which he bases his action
as explicitly shown in the statement or there was colossal
bias. In the circumstances, it seems more charitable to
accept the former view.

1. The Governor, with apparent emphasis on certainty
says, 'I will describe briefly the regulations I have made
for you after I have told you with utmost frankness the
full reasons that have led me to take this action.'

After this, he goes on to speak about the Accra Conference; he describes how Mr Nkumbula (President of the
only African political party that has *not* been banned in
Central Africa) 'disagreed with certain things and left
before the Conference had ended'. The poor man does not
know that if Mr Nkumbula disagreed with certain things
then he did so in deep silence that could only mean consent.

Let Mr Nkumbula be called to prove that he disagreed with certain things and explicitly said so. To say
that Mr Nkumbula left the Conference before it ended
is as true as it could be to say Governor Benson has been
the doctor in charge of the African Hospital in Lusaka
for the last five years. Mr Nkumbula left Accra on
19 December 1958, on the same Pan American plane as
did Mr Tom Mboya, the Chairman of the Conference, Dr
Hastings K. Banda of Nyasaland and other delegates. I
was at the airport to see them off. I remember I spoke to
him about the 'Charter of Unity' that we signed in Accra
advising him not to do anything about it until my arrival
home. I remained behind because I accepted an invitation
extended to all delegates from the Extra-mural Depart-

ment of the University College of Ghana to attend a 10-day New Year School. Before going to the College I visited the Republic of Togoland for three days to see for myself what was happening there.

2. The next thing the Governor dwells upon to support his banning of Zambia is that the Accra Conference varied our usual pledge of non-violence to one of violence. This is not true because non-violence was the most emphasized word right through the Conference. Russell Howe writing for the *Sunday Times* had this to say:

'The All-African People's Conference which begins here on Monday is meant to produce a strategy for independence for each of the still colonized areas of Africa according to delegates from French and British West Africa. Apart from *non-violent* campaigns (the italics are mine) for independence the Conference will discuss the forming of economic and political Federations of the 'United States of West Africa' type; proposed revision of certain African frontiers, most of which were arbitrarily fixed at the Berlin Conference in 1884 and often present certain ethnic anomalies; the future position of chieftaincy, traditional religion and "tribal" organizations; the status of African women and other social questions.'

This, in actual fact, is the line that was followed at the Conference. The Governor's source of information here again is as faulty as in 1 above.

3. The Governor goes on to say inter alia: 'It is the Zambia leaders who have, since the turn of the year, been threatening violence to other Africans, been declaring that Africa is for Africans alone, been organizing disobedience to just laws, and have in particular been making preparations to prevent by violence and intimidation any African voter from casting his vote at the elections on 20 March. This they have done openly in public. But worse, far worse, is what they have done privately in the villages and

in the towns at night. There they had instituted a reign of terror. They have placed men in fear of their lives. They have threatened death and mutilation to their wives and children. They have invoked witchcraft and unmentionable cursings in order to deter Africans from voting. And because all these things take place in private and at night with no witnesses, they are desperately difficult to deal with in law.'

From here, this Excellency goes on to compare us with Chicago racketeers. It is amazing that the highest representative of the Queen in the land will make such serious charges against us and when he is required to prove his allegations, he ends up by saying '. . . they take place at night and in private with no witnesses, they are desperately difficult to deal with in law'. I wish here Mr Commissioner to record my deep regret that this particular Excellency will not be here to prove his allegations.

I then went on to record the activities of the Zambia African National Congress which aimed at majority rule; 'in the same way as the English rule England, the French rule France, Japanese rule Japan, Indians rule India, Africans MUST RULE Africa'. I emphasized how unfair it was for the Governor who had all the opportunities of radio and press at his disposal to use the provincial administration, the police and many others to spread his propaganda and after failing to justify his action in banning and prosecuting us to say 'they are desperately difficult to deal with in law'. But perhaps this paragraph best sums up my argument:

Now the crowning reason why Sir Arthur acted as he did was his own fear of Zambia. Zambia grew almost overnight. Its influence was considerable. Its campaign against the Benson constitution was so intense and effective that Sir Arthur feared we were going to succeed in persuading our people to stay away from polling stations on 20 March. Our success would have resulted in a constitutional crisis. Since this was his own constitution, he was naturally worried and had to do all in his power to make the constitution work. He did something and this was to ban Zambia, arrest and rusticate all its leaders.

I wish to state here categorically that we shall untiringly attack systems that for reasons of race alone deny about three million Africans the full enjoyment of democratic rights in this country. But I shall always pray that no bitterness shall come into the picture and that we freedom fighters shall be for ever colour-blind. We make no apologies for being in the forefront in the struggle for national independence and self-determination. FREEDOM IS OUR BIRTHRIGHT and we simply are determined to achieve it.

With this I beg to submit, sir, that the action taken by His Excellency, the Governor, Sir Arthur T. Benson, was uncalled for, unjust and wrong; and that not only should the ban on Zambia be lifted immediately but that an apology be made to us on behalf of the Governor for his statement which is libellous.

Finally, I wish to make this appeal to you that you recommend the setting up of a Constitution Commission to enquire into the establishment of a democratic constitution based on ONE MAN ONE VOTE as this is the only way to end political strife in this our MOTHER LAND.

15

Prison

I remember one day telling Frank Chitambala that he should go through all his files to find out whether there was anything objectionable that the police might use against him. I don't now remember whether he took my advice seriously but the following morning I received for the first time a nice letter from the D.C. inviting me to go and have a chat with him. Both Frank and Musonda accompanied me. On arrival at the Boma office, I was rearrested and taken back to my Kabompo home for a thorough search. Unfortunately, I had not taken any breakfast that morning. We drove from Kabompo to Balovale only to learn that our friends and colleagues had also been searched. I took it for granted the search had been country-wide, and this was, in fact, the case. At Balovale, the kind wife of the C.I.D. officer offered me some orange juice and that was the only food I took till very late in the night.

I urged my temporary custodians to be quick so I could get to Lusaka in time to contact my lawyers. They told me both of them were away. I learnt later this was not true. The truth is that they had orders to land at Lusaka airport at 7 p.m. On arrival, someone else drove me to the Central Prison, Lusaka. I went back to my old familiar cell where in 1955 I had lived with Mr Nkumbula. This time the beds had not been removed; in fact, there were bed sheets, two

piilows and two pairs of pyjamas. I had some bread, marga-
rine and cheese that night. The following morning my
lawyer came and we sat together to prepare my case. We
did not refuse the charge and so I prepared to give a
long statement which the presiding magistrate ruled out
as a political speech before I could finish reading it. My
lawyer gave the Crown witnesses a very hard time and,
finally, I was given nine months on the first count which was
'conspiring to effect an unlawful purpose' and I got three
months on the second count which was 'authorizing to be
held an unlawful meeting'; the sentences to run concur-
rently. On one occasion during my trial the police officer
who was taking me to the court became annoyed with me
for waving back to our people who waved when they saw
me. He said to me, 'Why do you keep waving all the time as
if you were Elizabeth the Queen Mother? If this continues,
I will see to it that you come to court in the Black Maria –
do you understand?' Of course I understood, but I did not
say so. I continued to wave but this time very carefully. The
idea of travelling by a Black Maria was not a very pleasant
prospect. Munukayumbwa Sipalo who had been rusticated
at Feira was also in prison with me but he was not living
with me at the European, Asian and Euro-African quarters.
He was kept at what is called 'The Confinement', obviously
to keep us apart.

My morning began at 6 a.m. At this time, the arrival of
the superintendent would be heralded by deafening noises
caused by the opening of the gigantic locks of the two doors
south of my own. Mine would then be opened. Almost without exception, the African warder would quietly greet me
respectfully and then retreat to the door. As soon as he was
certain the European officer would hear him, he would raise

With Mr Joshua Nkomo and Mr Iain Macleod during the London talks, 1961

With the Tanganyika representative Mr Ngaiza, Sir Stewart Gore-Browne and Mr Desai. On the left is Mr Wina

Our delegation at the United Nations Special Committee, April 1962. *l. to r.*, Mr T. L. Desai, Sir Stewart Gore-Browne, self, and Mr A. N. L. Wina

his voice and make some queer sound with his incredibly big bunch of keys by rubbing it against the door and then shout in a terribly harsh voice, *Vuka, vuka, vuka,* meaning, 'Wake up, wake up, wake up'. The European officer would then come in and take a quick look round my room and then ask, 'Everything all right?' and I would reply, 'All right thank you, Officer.' As cook for our European, Asian and Euro-African Section, I would then dash to 'warm up the stove' as we used to say. Our breakfast varied according to tastes. I would prepare something like this: tea or coffee, mealie meal and porridge, and then I would start cleaning pots, pans and plates. As everybody else would be parading to go out to work, I would then start on polishing floors. The superintendent usually came at about 9 a.m. for his round-up. By the time he came to my domain, it would be about 10 o'clock. He, like all of his kind, had a very sharp eye for anything dirty. I usually kept everything clean and then he would make suggestions as to what should be done. Such were in fact orders. If he was satisfied, he would say, 'Yes, keep it clean, Kaunda' in a heavy, slow voice in which one discerned satisfaction mixed with a feeling that there was still room for improvement. There was another officer whom I remember well. He was a Scotsman. He was a very frank man in performing his duties. He would say to me, 'Yes, keep singing your days out, Kaunda' as almost invariably he found me singing to myself when working. After his round-up, he would tell me with satisfaction he had never seen the kitchen so clean before. I would then thank him for his remarks and then he would leave. But he also had a very sharp eye for prison tricks. As for my fellow-prisoners, I cannot remember a single prisoner who was not on good terms with me in our section. We got on very well.

Some were gentle and repentant. Very apologetically they would say to me they realized I was not in for the same reasons as they were. I could see they were trying to comfort me although I needed no comforting at all.

There were also the beyond-redemption types. These would boast of their big exploits as the rest of us sat listening. I remember one of this type telling us he was suffering because of his connections with some gold mines in Southern Rhodesia. But when the truth came out it was discovered that our friend was doing his ninth sentence for house-breaking. These, as can be seen, are very sad human problems that require our sympathy more than anger.

Our lunch hour came between 12.30 and 2 p.m. There was meat for my section mates and fish for me. We also received vegetables, rice, beans, condensed milk, cheese and golden syrup. According to existing regulations I received four ounces less of sugar, cheese and fish than my white and brown counterparts. Shortly after lunch, I was ordered to clean our primitive bucket lavatory and then I would start preparing our evening meal which was in the main no different from our lunch. At 5.30 p.m. I would start pacing up and down our courtyard and then I would see, as some guards or late-coming prisoners opened the small door, a bit of the outside world – the green or brown of nature. Otherwise the only bit I saw of the outside was some branches of a *muwombo* tree (it is a fibre producing tree) which was just behind my cell and I could see it as I paced to and fro in our courtyard. I have also some vivid memories of a little friend which had no knowledge of me. This was a small aeroplane which flew over our prison almost every Sunday. At about 4 p.m. I would stand in the courtyard waiting to wave at it. I think it must have belonged to some Lusaka flying club. There were also some very friendly magpies which came to greet us when most of our friends from the African section had gone to their cells. These birds would come very close to us as if to say to us, 'We bring greetings from outside.' As soon as the guards came they flew out as if to say 'these we cannot trust'.

I was not allowed to speak to any other African prisoner and for that matter any African warder, except those on duty in my section. But in prison one learns to speak all sorts of languages; there is the normal spoken one and then there are hand, finger, eye, head and leg languages. So when I got up the first morning in Lusaka Prison, my fellow black prisoners who wanted to greet me used mainly these unspoken or symbol languages which are very difficult for anyone to detect. In prison, information services among inmates is first class. The spirit of oneness between them is admirable unless they are rivals or don't see eye to eye over something. Although there does exist some form of friendship between guard and prisoner, it depends on circumstances. A terrific amount of blackmail goes on. If, for instance, a warder is terribly cruel to his gang, he is likely to find himself in a position where he has been manœuvred into some difficulties out of which it is wellnigh impossible to extricate himself. On the other hand, warders have a way of putting their worst personal enemies among prisoners in some pretty sticky spots. As a result, there is very often an equilibrium of mutual respect struck between the two sides. If this does not happen, then trouble is to be expected.

I was just beginning to settle down to do my nine months in the Central Prison, Lusaka, when one of my informants warned me that I was being moved to the Central Prison in Salisbury. The following morning, four of us were picked up by the superintendent and made to dress in our own clothes. I was handcuffed to Wilson Chakulya who had been given sixteen months for a charge of sedition. He was Secretary of our Broken Hill district as well as General Secretary of the Central African Road Service Union of Workers. Munukayumbwa Sipalo was handcuffed to a man called Chirwa who had been given twenty years for alleged derailment of a train somewhere near Lusaka. The journey between Lusaka and Salisbury was uneventful. We travelled second class because we were told there were no European passengers on the bus. The countryside had changed from the beautiful green of the rainy season to the brown of July. I enjoyed this very much. Probably it was the confinement within the prison walls coupled with my Kabompo love for nature that made me pay so much attention to the brown colouring on both sides of the road. Our first stop was at Chirundu. At our second stop, Karoi, we asked the guard to remove the handcuffs so that we could help ourselves but he refused and so we travelled like this up to Salisbury. We got to our new home rather late in the evening. It was the first time any of us had seen such a prison. There were some ten gates from the main entrance to my room. It is so gigantic that it would pass for a seat of higher learning except of course for its fantastic walls. Sipalo used to make us all laugh by saying this place was so horrible it would make the wildest elephant tame.

On arrival, we were given a room each in a wing that is used for the accommodation of sick people and those in transit. In the morning, we were issued with what is described as a superior uniform; regulation wear for Indians and Euro-Africans. We were then locked up in our respective rooms again. This made a good number of people very curious. I remember one prison officer coming along obviously anxious to find out what 'this trouble-maker' looked like. For some reason which I was never able to find out, he came dodging from one place to another, and my guess is there must have been instructions to all not to call on us until the top man had issued his orders. However, as my friend came dodging towards my door, I saw him through the usual pigeon hole through which warders speak to their prisoners. Because he was concerned with those outside, he did not notice I was watching him until he was about a foot from me and as soon as he realized I was watching him, poor fellow, he dived and went back this time in a straight line. Actually, he became a very helpful man to me in so far as my health was concerned in that prison.

When I reported at the office to meet the top man, he outlined to me how he expected me to behave. In fact, there was nothing out of the ordinary. I thought he was being very reasonable. As for work he directed that I should join the book-binding team.

Although we were working alongside non-political prisoners, some prison officers insisted we should not mix with any of them at any parades. One of the most difficult prison officers to deal with happened to be on duty on the second or third day of our stay there. As we were parading to go in he saw us standing about five yards away from the man at the end of the line of ordinary prisoners. Shouting at the top of his voice he said, 'KU – ANDA, get to the back and take him with you (meaning Sipalo) or else I will cut your legs off for you. And while doing so I shall be smiling just to show there is no actual animosity.' This man was ex-Kenya. He was in charge of the supply of things like toothpaste. He kept me for three solid weeks without supplying me with my much-needed toothpaste. I kept on complaining to the senior superintendent until he went in to order this officer to bring a tube of toothpaste to me. He was about twenty yards away from my cell when he started calling, 'KU . . . ANDA, KU . . . ANDA, KU . . . ANDA.' When I did not answer, he said, 'Where is this native they call Kuanda?' I then said, 'I am here, officer, how can I help you?' He came in and stared at me, his eyes full of anger. After he had satisfied himself he threw the paste at me. I said, 'Thank you.' He then replied to my thank you by saying, 'Don't thank me. I don't give toothpaste to natives – go and thank the senior superintendent.' I smiled back. He made faces at me and then went away.

Our morning began with breakfast. Because mealie meal porridge gave me so much stomach trouble, I took nothing when there was no brown bread in our stock of foodstuffs unless we had oatmeal which, of course, was very rare. I did not complain about this to the superintendent because he was so kind to us that very often we hesitated to approach him if we could avoid it. I remember that each time I thanked him for his good treatment, he would reply that he was only performing his duties. He always gave twice as much consideration as he was given by anyone else in prison. He said that by behaving the way he did towards us he was only being reciprocal. But with the exception of the very top few, most of his subordinates took an entirely different view. They tried to harass us as much as they could, but I think we succeeded in refraining from giving them the excuse they were looking for so that they could ill-treat us to their hearts' content. One day I remember we received an official visit from a Federal Minister. He did not come to our workshop but when his party was about thirty yards away, the senior superintendent called out for me. The Director of Prisons introduced me to the Minister who said that we had never met before although both of us came from Northern Rhodesia. He added, 'I understand you have been a model prisoner here.' I thanked him and replied that I did not know about my being a model prisoner but that both the senior superintendent and the Director of Prisons might know. The senior superintendent then cracked a joke saying, 'This man is here, sir, because he conspired to blow up the British Empire.' The Minister replied, 'That should stand him in good stead for his future responsibilities.' Our short chat ended that way. I respectfully withdrew as they continued on their tour of inspection.

After breakfast, we went to parade in readiness for work. In prisons one goes about not knowing what to expect and this is worse when one is moved to a new prison. In Lusaka Prison, we were exempt from the terrible habit of being made to strip naked and then disgracefully jumping up and down by raising one of your legs to show you were carrying nothing in between your legs. It is a degrading custom that I have learnt came from the Republic of South Africa as are so many of the indignities that we suffer. White prisoners are as a matter of our established custom exempt from this operation. On our first day in Salisbury Prison, we had to play tough not only to defend ourselves but also for the peace of the prison because we knew that our countrymen were quite ready for a big physical battle, in spite of our pleading with them, should any warder attempt to strip us naked. Fortunately the senior superintendent was in his office so that when we objected, word got to him quickly and he ruled that we should be exempt. At least we were relieved for the time being. Two weeks after that we fell into wrong hands. One afternoon, a white warder whom we had never seen before came in and saw us passing by. He shouted at us and ordered us to stop to be stripped. We stood still but no warder came near us as almost all those present had come to know us. However, as Providence would have it the only senior African warder, (I don't remember his proper rank but I think he was a major), intervened and explained to this white warder that it was the senior superintendent's orders that we should not be stripped. The white warder muttered something and we were allowed to go on.

After our morning parade which was at 7 a.m. we went to our workshop. We were very happy to learn bookbinding, which was extremely interesting. Between 11 a.m. and 1 p.m. we would go to lunch and would knock off finally for the day at between 3 and 4 p.m. Then the rush would begin for we all had to be in our cells shortly before 5 p.m. We all had to rush because we had to put our stomachs straight for the night, for although we had our chamber pots it was not a very pleasant thought to be locked up for some fifteen hours in a stinking cell. However, we were fortunately sufficiently organized not to have such a mishap.

We did a tremendous amount of reading in prison. We made a special application to have extra hours for reading and the senior superintendent was kind enough to allow us an extra hour. Miss Joan E. Wicken, then of the Africa Educational Trust, arranged for me to receive lectures on elementary economics from Ruskin College. Mr George Loft of the Society of Friends helped us with a good collection of books from his library as well as from the U.S.A. lending library. We also got some from the Indian Assistant High Commissioner's lending library. A good number of friends like Commander Fox Pitt, Guy Clutton-Brock and many others sent us books on request which the authorities were kind enough to inspect and allow in, so much so that we had quite an impressive library, including those books we were allowed to borrow from our book-binding shop. From this angle, one could say it was a very useful time. Father P. J. Walsh who had helped me with so many books in Lusaka Prison also very kindly drove my wife and my sixth boy to Salisbury from Lusaka to come and see me. I was allowed to meet my wife in a room used by white and brown prisoners on similar occasions. Only one who has been to Salisbury Prison and has seen how black prisoners are made to meet their relatives can appreciate how thankful I felt that I was allowed to meet my wife in this way. I should here also mention the fact that a good number of letters from my friends from many parts of the world reached me for which I am still thankful up to this time. A letter from dear friends in prison is a priceless gem and most of them I still keep today. They have a special value.

One other occasion I remember was when we had our monthly cinema shows. This had a dual value. First, we enjoyed the shows themselves tremendously and secondly, those nights were shorter in that we were longer in the open air than usual and, in fact, on these nights we were able to see the sky at night; and seeing the sky at night and hearing the barking of dogs in the distance was and will continue to be a rare treat until those dreadful walls are removed. Prisons are dreadful places for anyone but they have their value for those of us who meddle in public affairs. There we see some of God's own children who need more care and attention than any others collected as often as courts of law sit. To me, these have a good case for demanding from us spiritual, moral and material care as much as a person struck down with acute pneumonia needs a physician.

The prison is what one might describe as the headquarters of the underworld. It is a collection of people who themselves are one of the most challenging problems to mankind. They are such a mixture one does not know how to describe them beyond saying they are a challenge to us. This is true of prisoners all over the world I believe. But the problem is made worse when the question of colour plays a dominant part in deciding what shall be done to help them.

Going to prison for one's convictions means going there for a purpose. Here are some of the most terrible things I was able to notice which could be put right if the authorities chose to do something about the situation.

I cannot understand any reason why political prisoners should be made to mix up with incorrigible criminals. British colonial officials will always argue that they have hardly any political prisoners because those that they imprison are those who have committed ordinary crimes. Well, take my own team to illustrate what I mean. Wilson Chakulya was in for sedition and so was Munukayumbwa Sipalo. I was in for conspiracy and authorizing to be held an unlawful assembly. All these are political offences even though mine could not by law be said to be political and yet all of us were mixed up with other prisoners. It may be a clever way for Government to get round this but the problem is so deeply human that it is not right for any responsible government to dodge the issue through legal quibbling.

In any war, prisoners of war are always kept by themselves. I consider that freedom fighters of our type are 'at war' with their 'political masters', the only difference is that it is not a shooting one. The fact that they do not organize to kill does not make them any less respectable as defenders of their own and their people's rights than soldiers who have been taught to kill their fellow-men. I realize that this type of argument in a world which is full of respect for violent activities while paying lip service to non-violence cannot be the most popular.

I have said that prison is the headquarters of the underworld. During the few months I was in Salisbury Prison, I had the terrible experience of seeing young boys of between fifteen and twenty come in as first offenders for a few weeks and by the time they went out they had graduated so well they came back just a few days after their first release for longer periods. How did this happen? When these poor boys come in for the first time they are so scared they respond very quickly to anyone offering them protection and in many cases they will need it. But then those who offer them this protection do so with terrible motives. If a boy tries to resist, his so-called protector arranges with others to thrash him so that by coming to the boy's protection at the right moment, he will submit to his unnatural desires. The organization of these incorrigibles is so effective that warders will either explicitly or implicitly approve of the action. From this time, the boy is treated like a 'housewife'. Food as well as many other requirements in ordinary life which find their way in prison, in spite of the strict rules, the boy now receives. This is true, of course, of some grown-up men who agree to play the role of women, and it applies equally to white prisoners from what I was able to observe and hear from those white prisoners who worked with us at book-binding. I am certain from my observation that most of the fights in prison arise out of jealousies over boys who are treated in this way.

During the evening, 'lectures' are given. Prisoners tell the most fantastic stories of their exploits. These are repeated often, at places of work, on Saturdays and Sundays, and at every opportune moment – so that they sink into the minds of these youngsters or grown-ups who might have come as political offenders. Of course, some of these fantastic stories are true and some are just fabrications of 'theories' with which 'the lecturer' would like someone else to experiment. In this way, decent society is losing more and more.

Is it beyond our reach to come to grips with this problem in a young country such as ours? I know that people trained to do this type of job have been at it probably burning oil long after midnight, but this does not stop laymen like myself discussing it. In fact, I am encouraged to take this issue in this way mainly because I am convinced that very little is being done to help. I am convinced, further, that many of these people whom I have myself here called incorrigibles are not altogether lost to normal society if genuine efforts could be made to save them. I realize too that one cannot do much when our society outside the prison walls is so soiled, in so far as Africans are concerned, that some of these Salisbury prisoners used to say plainly that they were better off where they were than outside. They would argue they could never hope to find work, they would be harassed by the police for passes, tax receipts, and many other things. A society that drives some of its citizens to think in this way is rotten and needs burying. Here we are guilty of a serious offence for which we are bound to pay heavily unless changes come quickly and an entirely different approach is made almost immediately to this problem. When I say this, I am not obsessed at all; I am basing my argument on facts and figures. Think of the thousands of boys and girls who don't find places at schools. What is there to stop them 'graduating' at this underworld 'university' by the thousand?

Having said so much about my observations of my fellow-men in prison, it is only fair that I should say a word or two on the activities of religious men and justices who came to visit us. From my observation, I could see that these men were sincere and meant to be of some help and I believe some of them went away with a feeling that they were helping their fellow-men who were less fortunate. But I am sorry to say very little was achieved by them. Every Sunday morning, clergymen came to help us spiritually. Only prisoners who wanted to attend services were allowed out of their dormitory cells and I think I am correct in saying that about 95 per cent came out. On our first Sunday, we noticed that there was a big gathering in a certain corner, far more than any of the other five or six groups put together. The man in charge had to shout to be heard. I thought that was a very popular church in prison. The following Sunday, the same corner was very much crowded but to my surprise there was a different man from a different church and on the third Sunday, noticing the same thing, a big crowd and yet a third clergyman from another church, we began to wonder what was happening. We found out later that it was not the popularity of any one church that was involved but simply that this was the sunniest corner of the prison yard. Any priest who chose such a place was bound to get a very good attendance. Whether or not the priests themselves knew this, I don't know. I don't even know which churches were involved but they were both black and white. The teaching that went on could perhaps have converted some of these people towards right thinking and right living and to their Lord and Master but Sunday after Sunday we sat and listened and I watched but could hardly see any change. Those whose behaviour was admirable almost invariably had come to prison as such. The question now is this: did these priests know that the people they were preaching to were not really receptive to the message? Is it not the task of the Christian church to take stock of its successes and its failures especially where sinners of that type are concerned? Is this what takes place in all other prisons? If the answer is a 'yes', then obviously something must be done about this.

With regard to visiting justices, most of these rare visitors during my two spells in prison left me with the impression that there was much to be desired here. I must say right away that those of us who knew what we were in prison for could get or expect help from these justices, but the person who needed their help most, the common man who feels lost in such a place, did not even get near them. In fact, he did not even know why they were there. These people could be a force for good if only they could come down to earth. I do not know how they handled white prisoners but I can only go by how they handled those of us who were educated and, therefore, deduce that white prisoners must have got much more attention. It might be argued that the question of great numbers of Africans in prisons at any given time accounts for the fact that white prisoners whose numbers are far less receive more attention and, by the same token, it could be argued that the same is the reason why the vocal and enlightened black prisoner receives some attention because he is not in such vast numbers. This is one of the many tragedies of modern societies. They tend to leave the weakest to fend for themselves. If any society has any right to claim a place amongst the modern enlightened societies surely it must be prepared to meet such human problems as this. The trouble here is that apart from half-hearted efforts or attempts by a badly financed department of social welfare, it seems to me that those in authority don't even know that this problem exists. I am convinced beyond doubt that some of these people could be saved if we could treat these moral and spiritual diseases with the seriousness physicians treat serious cases of pneumonia for, in both cases, people are dying. The difference is that in the one case they are dying physically and in the other, morally.

16

U.N.I.P. and the Church

On 18 December, I was told to get my clothes from the store-room for pressing. I knew something was in the offing. That evening or early in the morning, my mind is not very clear, I was told that I was going back to Northern Rhodesia. To begin with I was supposed to fly with a warder but as there was only one seat on the plane that day, Sir John Moffat was allowed to give me a lift back to Lusaka. We had a full corporal in the back seat of Sir John's car. I remember how once again the fullness of life came to me as on both sides of the road, for over three hundred miles, we had nothing but the green of our December. It is one of the most memorable drives of my life and I am grateful to Sir John Moffat who, by helping me in this way, exposed himself to the bitter public attack of Mr John Gaunt. It will be appreciated how much I feel about this because, for five full months, I had been shut off from all natural beauty. We stopped on the way for lunch and arrived in Lusaka late at night. I went back to my familiar cell. Nothing eventful happened except that I must mention, with thanks, some of the kind friends who came to visit me like the Rev. E. G. Nightingale, Father P. J. Walsh, some members of the Prison Aid Society, Mr Harry Franklin and, of course, countless numbers of my fellow Africans.

On 9 January, the great prison gates were flung open and I was met by my lawyer, a press man and a photographer. I was released a day earlier because the 10th was a Sunday and no releases are made on Sundays, and I at once issued the following statement:

'Freedom! All I am asking the Africans of Northern Rhodesia is that they should remain calm and patient; and should prepare themselves for the real non-violent struggle that lies ahead.

'The Zambia African Congress was banned, but there is no power to ban our desire to be free, to shape our own destiny. In this struggle for freedom, we will tell the present rulers to realize that the colour of man should not count; what should count is his behaviour. We, the African people of Northern Rhodesia, are out to get power not for its own sake, but because we believe that it is the solution to our problems.

'I am prepared to unite all Africans who have the welfare of their people at heart. I would support a leaders' round-table conference only if I were certain that such a meeting was not held merely to show the world that African leaders in Northern Rhodesia could come together; I would like to see real unity achieved.

'I am determined more than ever before to achieve self-government for Africans in this country. Detentions, imprisonments and rural-area restrictions will only delay, but will not stop us from reaching that goal, which should be reached this year, 1960.

'I repeat that the Africans of Northern Rhodesia must be patient. We will negotiate with the British government and the Governor here. I will demand constitutional changes now. I hear that the new Colonial Secretary, Iain Macleod, is a man of great understanding. I am certain he will be sympathetic.

'We shall soon be putting before him our constitutional proposals which will be framed at the forthcoming conference of the United National Independence Party on 31 January. It is time that power shifted from the minority group to the majority, and by this I mean universal adult suffrage which is popularly known as "one man, one vote".

'I am hopeful that this can be achieved through a non-violent struggle. I, therefore, ask you all to be calm, patient and non-violent. I know your grievances. I know you have been calm and patient for a long time, but that should not make you behave otherwise. Give us your undivided support and loyalty, and we, as leaders, will fight for the freedom which we rightly deserve in a non-violent way.'

I was out of prison. On 31 January, I was elected to the Presidency of U.N.I.P. unopposed, thanks to Brother Mainza Chona who kindly stepped down to the Deputy Presidency of the party.

As soon as I began to address public meetings, I found that the presence of Northern Rhodesian police at every meeting could easily lead to violence. On the last day of January 1960, I addressed an enthusiastic gathering of my supporters at Kabwata. Several times the police officer in charge of the tape-recording machine came up to the speaking dais to adjust the microphone or note the speaker's name. Each time he was greeted with shouts of disapproval from the crowd. At one point, an altercation broke out between the recording officer and some of my followers blocking his path to the dais. It was with the greatest difficulty that I managed to control the crowd but I kept insisting that our policy was one of non-violence. I remember saying, 'If, because of our policy, you are lifted in the air and thrown to the ground, say "Kill me, but I shall be free." I was determined to combine Gandhi's policy of non-violence with Nkrumah's positive action.

All the time I was aware of the terrible danger of some of the young extreme elements of my party getting out of control and causing riots. In any nationalist organization there are bound to be 'roughs and toughs' who want to force the pace, and a way must be found of dealing with them. I suppose the method used by the British Labour party is one of the best. There one finds all sorts of people who hold widely differing views on this and that subject. They all, however, respect the views held by the majority of their group. This is one of those arts we must develop here in African parties if our yearning for constitutional democracy is to come to stay. 'One man, one vote' is now our watchword. We should stress, and indeed do stress, the importance of this not only at general elections but also as the only rightful method of deciding issues even within our own parties. Once this is grasped, it follows that a well-disciplined party will make its decisions by its majority binding. This, of course, is assuming that those 'roughs and toughs' are in the minority. If, on the other hand, those 'roughs and toughs' go out of their way to disregard majority decisions, they should be disciplined accordingly.

Sir John Moffat at this time moved a resolution in the Legislative Council of Northern Rhodesia stating that opposition to Federation had increased and that it was clear the present form of Federation could not last, and called for an association of states likely to be acceptable to the majority of the people. His motion was defeated by 21 votes to 7. This convinced me more than ever that we would never get our freedom by fighting the battle within the Legislative Council under the constitution then existing. The fight would have to be carried on by building up a strong party to force constitutional changes.

I determined on out-and-out opposition to the Central African Federation. I was not against federation in principle but against the Federation which had been imposed on us. I refused to give evidence to the Monckton Commission. I gave my reasons for this decision in full in *Black Government?*, a book which I wrote at that time.

At the end of March, I wrote to the Secretary of State for the Colonies, Iain Macleod, setting out my reasons for wanting a change in the Constitution:

'We have already submitted our case for SELF-GOVERNMENT NOW, but I wish to sum up the case as follows:

1 THAT we do ask for the graceful transfer of power from minority groups to the majority not only because we believe it is the God-given right of any people to rule themselves but because we believe quite sincerely that if an atmosphere of racial harmony and peace which we need in order to develop and exploit our abundant natural resources, is to be created, the majority must rule.

2 THAT such government minority groups need not have any fears that their interests might be jeopardized because

when we say we believe that 'all men are created equal and that they are endowed with certain inalienable rights, among them LIFE, LIBERTY and the PURSUIT of HAPPINESS', we mean this applies to all men on earth regardless of their race, creed, etc. We have no intention of replacing the present form of oppression with one of our own. As a mark of our goodwill, we have proposed as an effective safeguard for minority groups, if we could not be trusted, the retention of the Governor, Chief Secretary, Finance Minister and Attorney-General. This in itself is sufficient evidence to show we mean to keep our word.

3 THAT note should be taken of the fact that what is happening in both North and South Africa is influencing the situation here greatly. What I mean here is the getting of independence by our fellow Africans in the Congo and Tanganyika. The fact that some of our people have got their fellow tribesmen and relatives in the Congo and Tanganyika quite naturally adds to the unrest. Nor does the shooting of innocent Africans by the Verwoerd government help matters.

4 THAT the spending of *only* ten days in Northern Rhodesia and ten days in Nyasaland is a slight on the leadership of Africans of Northern Rhodesia who believe in non-violent struggle. It is being interpreted to mean that the British government will only move when there is bloodshed. To clear this unfortunate interpretation of the Secretary of State's action which perhaps in normal circumstances could have been accepted quickly, I believe it is advisable for the Secretary of State to announce an earlier date than October this year for a round-table conference for constitutional talks to which all interested parties

should be invited. This will put the fears and anxieties of Africans at rest.

'Sir, allow me to end by saying that such myths as "plural society", "partnership" and "multi-racial society" have meant domination of our indigenous people by immigrant races. To us, who actually feel the physical and mental strains, these have come to mean a thin disguise for white supremacy.

'Sir, the task before the British government is to choose between establishing in good time, which means your moving now, a truly British way of life which means making every citizen of and above the age of 21 a source of power and thereby establishing a democracy in which all people shall be happy and in which indeed Britain shall remain a friend of the people OR pleasing minority groups, which means maintaining the *status quo*, with the inevitable result of bitter racial strife and Britain remaining an enemy of Africans for ever. In any case, I don't think it is possible to reverse the trend of events. The clock, and nobody knows this better than you do, if I may go by what you have said and done for other countries, cannot be put back any longer.

'We have shown that we are a patient and long-suffering people. We are humanitarians and have no time for the colour of a person. We respond favourably to the Christian concept of man. Because of this attitude of mind we are being supported by an ever-increasing number of European and Asian liberals, but they will not come out openly at present owing to the situation created by Sir Roy Welensky, the Federal Prime Minister.'

While I was determined to get the constitution changed the Europeans were determined to maintain the *status quo*. At Kitwe, at the beginning of March 1960, Mr John Roberts, the leader of the United Federal Party in Northern Rhodesia, said, 'I say now, and I have good grounds for saying it, that there is no desire or intention on the part of the British government to review the present franchise or Constitution during the life of the present legislature.' That meant for another four years. At the same time, the more extreme Europeans under the leadership of Mr John Gaunt were forming what they called the 'Northern Rhodesia Association'. More than 1,000 whites packed Lusaka's largest cinema and heard John Gaunt call upon them to 'fight for their rights'.

I had been invited to go to America and I determined to call on Iain Macleod to ask him to give us a new constitution. It was while I was in London that I received the terrible news of the death of a European woman, Mrs Burton, whose car had been burnt after a political meeting. Mainza Chona gave me the news while I was at a press conference. I was deeply shocked and could hardly find words to express myself. I said that I did not know who had done this thing, whether it was followers of my own party or unknown hooligans. Whoever it was, I deeply regretted it. When my words were reported in Northern Rhodesia, a member of the Legislative Council spoke of them as the 'antithesis of sincerity'. I have sometimes wondered whether I was doing any good at all by condemning violence publicly. If I remained quiet, I was told that I was condoning violence; if I spoke about it, I was told that I was insincere. Mr John Roberts, the leader of Welensky's party in Northern Rhodesia, commenting on my statement about the death of Mrs Burton, said, 'I am not the least bit impressed by mere public affirmations of non-violence. It is from U.N.I.P. meetings where hatred is preached that acts of lawlessness spring. It is at these meetings, many of which are held after beer drinks, that a state of mind amounting to hysterical frenzy is worked up among the listeners.' It is a very great temptation sometimes when one is spoken of in this way to ask what really would happen if we tried to use violence instead of all the time trying to prevent it.

At this time, it was comforting for me to know that some churches were speaking out openly against the Federation. Many missionaries had been hoodwinked by the talk of 'partnership' and believed that Federation would be good for us, but gradually many had come round to understand that we had been right all along in our suspicions. I was encouraged to read in the *Northern News* one day that five Copperbelt clergymen, and one layman, representing African membership within the United Church, made a blunt policy statement in which they said, 'It is our responsibility to help bring to a peaceful end the present form of Federation. We are as determined as the political groups to see the end of a form of government that rules without the consent of the majority, that imprisons people without trial and has done little to remove discrimination.'

The United Church claims the largest African Protestant Church following on the Copperbelt. Their statement unreservedly backed the Africans' quest for self-government.

The statement announced the Copperbelt African churches' own private boycott of the Monckton Commission 'because the terms of reference do not allow people to say what they want to say about the Federation'. The African Churches' Council merely sent the Commission a written protest, and declined to appear before it.

At this point, I should digress to give my views about the

Church and politics because this is a matter of the greatest importance for the future.

As I have already related, I was brought up in a Christian home and my Christian belief is part of me now. It is still my habit to turn to God in prayer asking for His guidance. I do not think I have ever seriously doubted the truth of the Gospel, but I seriously question sometimes whether God is really speaking to us in the voice of the organized churches as I see them in Northern Rhodesia today. There may be many good reasons why the Christian Gospel came to us in the form of the 'denominations' of the West, but I cannot see any good reason for those same denominations continuing in these days. We become more and more confused as new sects from the West spring up in our towns. How can I believe in the sincerity of Christians who, in Lusaka alone (European population 14,000), hold seventeen separate denominational services for Europeans every Sunday. This denominational idiocy is a terrible condemnation of Christianity and is a confusion to my people and to myself. In my days at Lubwa, I had begun to question certain things in the life of the mission which seemed incompatible with the teaching of Christ in the Bible. I could not see why the European missionaries should have special seats in the church and why the Rev. Paul Mushindo went about on foot or on a cycle while the missionaries rode around in cars.

I found myself wandering in a spiritual wilderness and I became very bitter, as the following extract from a letter which I wrote to the missionaries at Lubwa in March 1952 well illustrates. I had been reading Bernard Shaw's *Man of Destiny* and I wrote:

'When (the Englishman) wants a new market for his adulterated Manchester goods, he sends a missionary to teach the Natives the Gospel of Peace. The Natives kill the missionary, he flies to arms in defence of Christianity, fights for it, conquers for it, and takes the market as a reward from heaven.'

In spite of my early revolt against the missionaries, I knew that the Christian religion had something important to say to us in our political movement. We were always looking for Christians to support us in our struggle.

In March 1953 at the Congress Delegates' Conference at Kitwe, we had decided to call our people to observe two days of prayer to ask God to assist us in our struggle against Federation. The Churches, except the African Methodist Episcopal Church of course, ignored this, saying that the African National Congress had no authority to call people to prayer. Only the Governor should do such a thing. Each missionary took his own line of action illustrated by the completely different attitudes of two brothers. One at the Kafue Training Institute gathered with the staff for prayer on the occasion, while the other at Mumbwa had a teacher dismissed for being absent from work on that day. Our National President, Mr Harry Nkumbula, made a statement after the Day of Prayer in which he said:

'The two days of National Prayer are over. I must thank the observers of those days. It has been alleged by the government that the Congress has deliberately fixed these days for prayer to God in order to disrupt the country's economy. I must tell the government that this is a misunderstanding of Congress's plans. The Congress leaders decided to have these two days of National Prayer in order to pray to God for assistance in their struggle against Federation. The people were told to observe those days with great reverence and were asked to refrain from any activities which might lead to disturbance. I am indeed grateful for the co-operation of the people who observed the days.

'Apart from worshipping God, the days served as a testing case for the African Anti-Federationists and also to see what the reactions of the government and the employers would be. I must deplore the reactions of the government and employers to the days of National Prayer. The government instructed the employers to dismiss those who observed the days, and also to evict them from their quarters. I am sure I cannot be too far wrong in saying that the government intended to intimidate the Africans who are fighting against Federation, and also to incite the people against the Congress.'

In that year, 1953, we were deeply hurt by the imposition of Federation, and very sensitive to any attacks made on us. We believed sincerely that we were fighting in a righteous cause but the very churches which had taught us the meaning of the fatherhood of God and the dignity of man seemed to be against us in our struggle.

The Minutes of the Regional Pan-African Council held in the Ex-Askaris Memorial Hall on 10 and 11 December 1953 show clearly that we were at that time in no way opposed to Christianity. We invited Mr Meembe of the African Methodist Episcopal Church to our Conference and his address is reported in full in the Minutes. What he said is well worth mentioning for it refutes the accusation frequently made against us that we were anti-Christian racialists.

'We are all brothers, for we are all children of God, and we should work together. No man can hate his fellow man or try to stop his progress, or keep him from enjoying all the fruits and rights of his country and of salvation in Christ.

'While we are all children of our earthly parents by physical birth, we become by spiritual birth, in a special sense, the

148

children of God. And in that spiritual relationship, all men should live in peace and love. If people do not belong to our race, colour or nation we must not hate them, for we are all God's children, and God's children must work together to banish sin from the heart and not to work against one another.

'I believe this is the aim of this Conference of the Pan-African Council assembled here today. White and black should live and work together. Not white against black and black against white. MAY GOD BLESS YOU ALL.'

By 1957, we were fighting the Federal Franchise Bill and the Constitution Amendment Bill. I think we were all delighted that the Christian Council of Northern Rhodesia for once seemed to be in line with us.

We were encouraged by this evidence that the Church was on the march, and fully in agreement with the editor of the *African Times* who wrote, 'Never before has the Church in Northern Rhodesia been so bold as to speak out against Government when its policies and practices have been seen to violate Christian morality.' In a young country like Northern Rhodesia, churches have a big part to play in its development. They cannot hope to succeed by confining their work to church buildings.

Christian principles can never be split, they have either to be accepted, or sacrificed as they are. In our opinion, for Christian Churches not to condemn racial discrimination, whether practised by black or white governments, or any other groups, is to sacrifice Christian principles. What is immoral cannot safely be passed as Christianly right.

In 1960, I set out in the book *Black Government?* my views on the subject of Missions in the life of the country and I have no reason to change what I said then.

It is my firm belief that we need an increasing number of Christian men and women in all political parties. It was our good Lord who said that his disciples should be the salt of the earth, but I am sorry to say that many Christians are prevented from joining political parties. For example, many Christian teachers fear to join our U.N.I.P. openly because they fear that they will be put on a black list either by their missionary managers or by Education Officers. I get angry when the official Church tells me to control my people and prevent hooliganism but they do not raise any finger at all to encourage their people to take an active interest in our political movements.

One of the great difficulties is that the police in the towns do not give permission for political meetings to be held on Sunday afternoons. I am therefore forced to hold them on Sunday morning which interferes with Sunday morning worship. This puts a big strain on many of my good members who have to choose whether to attend my meetings or go to church.

I am now the member of no church and yet feel myself to be a member of every church. I have hardly any opportunity of attending public worship and all I can do is sometimes to read and pray in my house. I do not think the Church in Northern Rhodesia understands the terrible danger it is in. Because the Christian Church in this country has so often failed to practise what it preaches in the matter of race and politics, thousands of my fellow Africans have rejected it. Although as yet many have kept their faith in the Christian message, they and their children will also lose that if the Church is not seen to consist of people who carry the teaching of Christ into every part of life. I am always hoping the Church will put its own house in order because our new nation of Zambia needs thousands of true Christians at this time.

17

A Year of Decision

The first full party working committee of the United National Independent Party was called in August 1960 and I spoke at length to the delegates, setting before them our objectives and the methods we would use to achieve our aims. I warned them of the grim struggle which lay ahead: 'Today, you have Special Branch men and women following wherever you go as if you were criminals; today you stand the chance of being sent to jail for shouting slogans like "FREEDOM NOW"; today you are liable to be deported from your own home for the "offence" of telling your people this was their country and it was their birthright to rule themselves. This is where we stand today. The terrible stories that have been written about struggles in India, Egypt, Ghana, and other countries that were once upon a time ruled by Britain, are taking place right here. Sad though these things are, they serve one useful purpose and that is they all are a pointer to the fact that we are moving in the right direction. I wish to repeat what I said when in exile in Kabompo: that British imperialists never exile or imprison political fools.'

I told them that if we failed to organize for independence because we feared prison or exile, it simply meant we were not ready to take over. 'The white man lords it over us in all walks of life not because he happens to be white but because he is better organized than we are; that is his secret. Our task is now to mobilize all the forces that we can for *self-government now*. This is no small task at all. It means choosing your friends well here and abroad, it calls for sincerity of purpose, determination and courage, self-discipline. Indeed, it calls for the three Nkrumah "S's" – SERVICE, SACRIFICE and SUFFERING. Nothing can be achieved anywhere and in any field without good organization. For those who have succeeded in life good and effective organization were their watchwords. We are capable of organizing effectively here if only we can seriously put our heads together.

'To organize for anything effectively, you must have clear in your own mind what you want, and how you mean to get it. We of U.N.I.P. know what we want, self-government now, and we also know how to get it, through non-violent means plus positive action.

'When we organize our people, it is important to note that we are building an organization that should not only get us self-government and, ultimately, independence, but an organization sufficiently strong to run our government. Putting it briefly, we are organizing to bring into being here a government of the people, by the people and indeed for the people. We criticize and condemn the present set-up as undemocratic, unethical and entirely un-Christian and, therefore, unworthy of self-respecting people. It is a government of the privileged few, by the privileged few and for the privileged few. It is these few that the Welensky governments in Central Africa are arming. He is creating all-white battalions, in spite of the existing regiments which are mixed racially. All this should not surprise us, although we condemn it unreservedly, because it is part of the privileged few's organization in order to perpetuate here their rule of oppression and suppression.

'Now, in a situation like ours where the oppressor is armed to the hilt, the oppressed, before man discovered the comparatively new method of passive resistance, had either to succumb to oppression or come out in open revolt against it. History is full of such incidents. Succumbing to oppression is undignified and unworthy of any self-respecting man. On the other hand, open revolt often leads to the killing of countless people, those very people for whom freedom is sought. So we resort to the third method – the method of passive resistance or non-violent methods plus positive action. It is easy to succumb to oppression and grumble silently. It is, of course, less difficult to organize an open revolt, but it is more difficult to organize a non-violent struggle in that it calls for conviction on the part of all participants. This type of movement obviously calls for extensive coaching and very often results come after a long time, and this needs much more discipline than an open revolt. But the fruits of this training stand the participants in good stead when they take over the reins of government. This is the method we have chosen. We have no intention at all of making our people cannon-fodder for colonialist guns.'

It was not the first time that this method had been used in Northern Rhodesia. I reminded them of the first non-violent struggle for social reform and the sense of pride and self-respect engendered in all who participated. It puzzled those who were armed to meet non-violence with violence. They had no alternative but to send those simple but self-respecting ordinary but spiritually newly-born black men, women and children to prison. It was indeed very moving and memorable to see humble people choose to go to prison rather than buy meat through pigeon-holes and stand exposed to all natural forces in long queues. British prisons were filled from Livingstone to Abercorn, and from Fort Jameson to Chingola. This wonderful campaign was organized between 1953 and 1957 to effect a measure of social reform.

At meetings up and down the country I repeatedly stressed the need for a well-lubricated party political machine. Every single member of the party must be kept in constant and close touch with party headquarters. The party must become the trusted mouthpiece of all the people, so that each and every one would be ready to suffer, if necessary, together, in the cause of freedom. This kind of solidarity was even more necessary after independence had been achieved.

No organization of any type, industrial, social or political, can survive without discipline. It brings self-control, and is of the utmost importance in a political party. Both leaders and ordinary members must submit to it, but the leaders particularly, must set a good example. They are closely watched by their followers and much depends on how they conduct themselves. In a campaign employing methods of non-violence, discipline is even more vital, especially when the tide of nationalism is rising all the time.

By the end of 1961, Mr Iain Macleod was urging my party to attend the Federal Review Conference in London. I went unwillingly because I could see no point in reviewing a Federation which I and my party was committed to destroy. As I expected, this conference achieved nothing; however, it gave me the opportunity to continue the pressure for a conference to review our Northern Rhodesian constitution. This conference which finally met in London was boycotted by the United Federal Party, but it was there that Iain Macleod first proposed the now famous three-fifteen plan.

We went to the London conference believing that we had the support of the Northern Rhodesian Liberal Party led by Sir John Moffat for our claim for an African majority in the next Legislative Council. Right at the end of the conference, Mr Macleod seemed to do a deal with the Liberal Party behind our backs. We were bitterly disappointed and it was then that I issued what has come to be known as my 'Mau Mau' statement. This needs some explanation because it is still quoted against me.

On 9 February 1961, I issued a statement headed, MY PEOPLE ARE TIRED, in which I warned that should Welensky and the British government continue to frustrate the legitimate aspirations of the African people of Zambia, a mass rising might result in Northern Rhodesia which would make Mau Mau seem a child's picnic.

As far as I was concerned, Mau Mau meant not only a massacre of white people by black people, but also a massacre of blacks by whites. Over the previous months, the Europeans of Northern Rhodesia, encouraged by Welensky and his Northern Rhodesian leader, John Roberts, had been behaving in a manner likely to cause tension and crisis. Troops had openly carried arms in the streets. The gun shops on the Copperbelt were doing a roaring trade in firearms to the European population. Had my people not behaved themselves more decently than the whites, a single incident could have resulted in mass shootings of Africans by panicky white settlers. Would not then Mau Mau have looked like a child's picnic? With only this difference, that instead of mass graves for whites, we would have been having mass graves for blacks.

As soon as the results of the London conference were made known, Welensky and Greenfield, his clever Minister of Law, got to work and by some kind of back door diplomacy managed to get the plan changed in favour of the United Federal Party. In June, the Governor of Northern Rhodesia announced a constitution which came as a bitter shock to us all. When I first read the White Paper, I could hardly believe my eyes. I had always told my people to trust the British government, and I personally had great regard for Iain Macleod. Now we had been deceived once again and we were very angry. Even the Christian Council of Northern Rhodesia which was meeting at Kitwe in June just after the new proposals were announced was moved to pass a Resolution which stated:

'The Council consider that the present proposals for the Northern Rhodesian Constitution will intensify racial antagonisms and thereby fail to provide the basis for the building of that orderly non-racial society which is the earnest desire of the Christian Church, and that they are, therefore, a burden on the Christian conscience because it is clear that the proposals are unacceptable to the great majority of the people.'

The Annual Conference of U.N.I.P. had been called to meet at Mulungushi on 9 July. There we denounced the new proposals and I knew that the time had come to start positive action. The British government had taken advantage of my reasonableness and had given way to pressure from the Federal government.

There were 3,000 people at that conference, every one of whom was deeply angered by what had been done to us.

They wanted action immediately and I have never before been so conscious of the latent force of anger in a people. Strangely enough, I myself felt a deep peace. The crowd did not want to listen to me when I urged on them the absolute necessity for our struggle to remain non-violent. Had I at that moment departed from my belief in the power of non-violence, I dare not think what bloodshed would have taken place in our land.

I told members of the conference to go and tell our Chiefs and people that our would-be protectors had succumbed to pressure from Welensky in Salisbury, and to Lord Salisbury and Tory back benchers, in order to maintain their ugly Federation. 'The British government has betrayed us; they have sold us down the cold river of white supremacy in the same way as their predecessors did in the Union of South Africa about fifty years ago. They are treating us like pieces of dirt. Shall we any longer trust them? At least my trust in them is finished. In my own mind's eye, I can still see Mr Macleod's face. It is a trustworthy face in so far as I am able to discern faces and read other people's minds. Many fellow-colonial leaders have told me the same about him. What then has gone wrong with him over Northern Rhodesia? He has made no efforts to meet our demands for a clear African majority. Instead, he gives us something unparalleled in colonial history. The British prime minister lectured us about 'noble principles', 'goodwill between races' and the importance of the 'give and take' spirit. All he meant was that we should be principled, and not Welensky; goodwill between men of all races should come from us only and not Welensky; and that in this spirit of give and take we should do all the giving while Welensky does all the taking. I am afraid I am a most shocked and disappointed man. We are being sacrificed at the altar of foreign politics. They gave in to Welensky in order to save Whitehead's referendum which means saving Welensky himself and, therefore, saving the Federation at the expense of our political advancement; the very thing successive colonial secretaries have assured us would not happen. Does this way of behaving call for any more trust? I have said already, mine is shaken to the foundation. The big question is, where do we go to from now?

'I know full military and police preparations are going on in the Union of South Africa, in this rotten Federation of Rhodesia and Nyasaland, in Angola and Mozambique. I know too that military pacts are being made between these three foreign powers to try and entrench their governments on the soil that is not theirs. They can claim to have lived here since 1400. The fact still remains, this is African soil. It is here we are born; it is here we die. Countrymen, this is a fitting moment for me to say like Shakespeare, 'Our legions are brim full, our cause is ripe.' U.N.I.P. has become a most powerful organization because each member has played his part honestly, sincerely, truthfully, and untiringly; and because we have based our policy on humanitarian principles. The battle still remains the same. It is not anti-white, but anti-wrong. We have many friends among men of all races. We shall not fight against white racialists and at the same time be racialistic ourselves.

'Nor will we lose our sense of direction. To our European friends and comrades in the struggle, I say yours is not an easy task either. You will meet with many difficulties. You will be ostracized in your own community and you will be doubted by the very people you like to associate with. But knowing as you do that the course you have chosen is the right one, you will stick to your guns and continue to show other people, misled by wrong principles, that peace here can only come when the principle of African majority rule is established. I don't envy your position at all but you have my blessing.

'To our Asian friends and comrades in the struggle, I say you know what we are trying to do. You faced it in your countries of origin. You know we are doing the right thing. Most of you are also men of principle. You have openly supported us.

'To our Euro-African people, we say we welcome you as members of our society. For some time you were misled by the powers that be. You discovered their trick of divide and rule. You came back to where you truly belonged and belong. They are now beginning to make attempts to separate you once again; to tempt you into falling an easy prey to their propaganda. You know the truth. You will no doubt stick to your beliefs.

'I have repeatedly asked the people of Northern Rhodesia to be patient and non-violent in thought, word and deed. But I have recently had to remove one of these noble words from my vocabulary. It is 'patience'. Welensky refused to be patient, and he got what he wanted. We who were patient have been neglected.

'The time has now come for us to show even more discipline in carrying out our policies. We will have to act in a positive but non-violent way.'

The days that followed the Mulungushi Conference were anxious days. Most of the country remained peaceful but in the Northern Province the long years of frustration spilled over into violence. In went the mobile unit of the Northern Rhodesian police and the white troops of the Federal army. Schools were burnt down, whole villages were gutted by fire; about eight Africans were killed in various incidents by the security forces of Welensky's army. No one more than I regrets the violence that took place in the Northern Province, but if you drive an animal into a corner and torment it, you may expect that in its fear and rage it will slash back at you.

There are always those who say that violence pays and that it was what happened in the Northern Province that made the British government once again change its mind. It is not for me to say what goes on in Whitehall, all I know is that now in 1962 we have been given a constitution in which we have decided to work for majority rule in Northern Rhodesia. For the first time in our history we may be able to use the ballot box to break up this ugly Central African Federation.

For a long time I have led my people in their shouts of KWACHA (the dawn). We have been shouting it in the darkness; now there is the grey light of dawn on the horizon and I know that Zambia will be free.

APPENDIX I

To understand, or even to begin to understand our troubles of today one must go right back into history and start with what was known as the Partition of Africa, or more colloquially, the Scramble for Africa. It has been well described in the following words:

The closing years of the nineteenth century were marked by an advance of the white races upon the continent of Africa which in its circumstance was a unique phenomenon in history. This invasion was the product of forces over which governments have little control, and which it is not easy to identify. Two phenomena may be suggested. One was the passion for adventure which expressed itself in the cosmopolitan stream which flowed continuously into and through Africa – a flow in which scores of men risked, and in the majority of instances ultimately sacrificed, their lives to the ardour of discovery.

The other phenomenon was the slave-raiding horror which the reports of Livingstone and his contemporaries in the '60s and '70s first made vivid to the Christian public. Cynical commentators have doubted the genuineness and extent of the revolt of conscience which was roused by the revelation of preventable human agony on a vast scale. But its reality was witnessed to by the stubbornness of resolve which it engendered. A multiplicity of individual motives, mingled of every shade of selfishness and altruism were combined in the culminating initiation of the onrush; the urge of trade, the ardour of evangelization, the love of gain, the pride of empire, the conscious trusteeship of civilization, the jealousies of patriotism. Its continuance was inevitable from the moment

161

that contact was fully established between races so far apart in the scale of progress.[1]

Those words, from the biography of the fifth Marquess of Salisbury, the British prime minister to whom the major credit for preventing the Partition of Africa from provoking a European war is mostly due, go far to explain what has been called 'the most perplexing yet important problem in the world today, the friction and conflict arising from the close contact of two or more communities, each with differing patterns of culture, within the same political entity'.[2]

As a matter of fact the vast inland territory which is now Northern Rhodesia was not affected by the scramble at first. No organized movement either of trade or evangelization reached it at first. But 'it was a tragic immunity. North of the Zambezi these lands had long been a favoured hunting ground for Arab slave raiders. Whole villages had been swept away – wide reaches of territory had been depopulated – and it would be hard to fix upon any spot in the habitable globe whose standards of well-being would not have borne favourable comparison with this sanctuary of independence.'[3] Lord Salisbury himself was anxious for the two Rhodesias and Nyasaland to become an Imperial Protectorate under the Foreign Office, 'but the obstinate dislike of the British Treasury to any further adventures which would increase the responsibility and the yearly expenditure of Great Britain'[4] prevailed, and in 1891 the lands north of the Zambezi, now Northern Rhodesia, were formally placed under Cecil Rhodes's Chartered Company.

At this time the four main warrior tribes which had invaded the territory from the north-west and the south were all pretty

1. Lady Gwendolin Cecil, *Life of Robert Marquess of Salisbury*, Vol IV, p. 222.
2. E. Clegg, *Race and Politics*, p. 1.
3. op.cit., p. 240.
4. Sir Harry Johnston, *History of the British Empire in Africa*, p. 122.

well established in the areas where their descendants are now living. They were the Bemba, the Barotse, the Lunda, and the Ngoni; the last-named having crossed the Zambezi as late as 1833. Inter-tribal warfare was frequent, and the raiding of the smaller, weaker tribes which surrounded them seems to have been incessant. The Arab slave-traders played their gruesome part, and when they were not raiding on their own behalf, exchanged cloth and guns for prisoners taken in war.

All four tribes are of Bantu origin, and in spite of many differences with each other have much in common. Thus the Bemba and the Barotse are matrilineal, and the Ngoni patrilineal, but all have the same approach to land problems, holding that all members of the tribe have the right to cultivate. All have similar religious beliefs, a form of ancestor worship. None of the tribes have a written language, all have a firm belief in magic and witchcraft. Like all human beings they have a mixture of good and bad qualities. Where perhaps the conditions under which they have lived are most likely to produce conflict with the Europeans with whom they come in contact is in their attitude to continuous labour, which forms little or no part of their tribal training. Dr Richards, in her monumental work, *Land, Labour, and Diet in Northern Rhodesia*, calculates that under tribal conditions amongst the Bemba the necessary labour required to maintain the community only occupies its members for about seven months in any year.

To return to the early history of Northern Rhodesia, when the territory came under the Chartered Company in 1891 it was nominally administered by Sir Harry Johnston, Her Majesty's Commissioner for Nyasaland, but actually he was too much occupied with suppressing the slave-trade in the latter country to be able to spare time, or men, from his small force, which consisted at first of only 70 Sikh soldiers from India, 80 Zanzibaris, two gun-boats lent by the Admiralty, and a mission steamer.

However, communications between Lakes Nyasa, Tanganyika,

and Mweru, were maintained, and small fortified stations con-
structed at Abercorn, and Fort Rosebery. By 1896 the Yao slavers,
the Arabs, and the Ngoni in Nyasaland, had all been defeated,
and the company began to operate in Northern Rhodesia. The
Bemba had up till then been left severely alone, but the defeat
of the slavers in Nyasaland had cut off their supply of arms and
ammunition, and after a few minor engagements with the company's native police force, which was officered by Europeans,
they submitted. The defeat of the Ngoni in the Fort Jameson
district by troops from Nyasaland, and of Kasembe's Lunda,
ended all hostilities in north-eastern Rhodesia. In north-western
Rhodesia Lewanika, King of the Barotse, who was anxious for
an ally against the Matabele, had signed the 'Lochner Treaty'
as long ago as June 1890, and no fighting took place.[1] By the
end of the nineteenth century Northern Rhodesia was effectively
pacified.

Two outstanding events have occurred in the present century
which have helped to make the Northern Rhodesia we know today. The first was the introduction of a Native Tax in 1900 in
north-eastern Rhodesia, and in 1904 in north-western Rhodesia.
The sum demanded from individuals was small, but the total
obtained was considerable, £57,000 out of the total income of
Northern Rhodesia in 1910-11. Much more important from the
point of view of racial contacts, it was the imposition of this tax
which compelled the tribal African to leave his village and go
away to find work, sometimes as far off as Southern Rhodesia,
or South Africa. The effect of this needs no explaining or
emphasizing. The other happening occurred many years later,
and was the opening up of the Copperbelt as we know it today,
which began in 1928 and culminated in the Territory becoming
in 1953 the biggest producer of copper in the world. It is now
the third biggest. In 1958 the value of copper produced was
£70,141,287. The wages paid to Africans amounted to
£6,318,573. During 1958 the mining industry provided employ-

1. L. H. Gann, *Birth of a Plural Society*, pp. 65–79.

ment for 7,350 Europeans and 39,780 Africans.[1] These figures speak for themselves.

Finally what has the political background been? For many years after the pacification of Northern Rhodesia the government of the country was entirely in the hands of European officials in all respects. And even when the imperial government took over from the Chartered Company in 1924, and replaced the settlers' Advisory Council by a Legislative there was still an official majority, and at the head of everything a Governor who was all-powerful in every respect. Africans had neither votes nor representatives. It is true that in 1929 an alleged form of indirect rule was introduced for the tribal areas which was supposed to strengthen the position of the Chiefs whom the Chartered Company had entirely ignored. But at this very time the development of the copper mines was drawing away thousands of Africans from the rural areas, weakening the power of the Chiefs, and destroying the very customs it was the intention of Government to protect.

During the same period the Europeans, settlers and traders, remained reasonably placid in the expectation that in due course they would receive self-government on Southern Rhodesian lines. But in 1930 Lord Passfield, the Labour Secretary of State, issued a statement of Native Policy, based on the statement issued in 1922 by the Tories, which contained the words: 'His Majesty's Government think it necessary definitely to record that the interests of African Natives must be paramount, and that if and when those interests and those of the immigrant races should conflict, the former should prevail.'

From that moment onwards amalgamation with Southern Rhodesia became the heartfelt desire of the great majority of un-official Europeans in Northern Rhodesia, until the day when Mr Welensky, the leader of the Northern Rhodesian unofficials became convinced, in 1946, and in his turn convinced Sir Godfrey Huggins, Prime Minister of Southern Rhodesia, that amalgama-

1. *Handbook of Rhodesia and Nyasaland*, pp. 64–5, 466–7.

tion would never be permitted by either of the two main political parties in Britain. Federation followed in due course, and at first anyhow, it was supported by a good many people who thought, and hoped, that, while avoiding the bad side of amalgamation, it would have considerable economic and administrative advantages.

African opposition to Federation was practically universal. The mistrust of Southern Rhodesia had become by this time almost pathological, and nothing in the way Federation was presented helped in any respect to weaken this feeling, rather it increased it.

Nevertheless in the pre-Federation years African political advance had not been entirely negligible. It is only necessary to chronicle the formation of African Provincial Councils, since abolished without any reason being given, and the African Representative Council, also now done away with (not to mention the fact that by the time Federation was seriously thought of there were African members of Legislative Council), to realize that there had been a marked change of attitude on the part of many Europeans towards Africans which it would be unfair entirely to discount.

So much for the past.

For the future one thing stands out, and that is that things have got to change. Perhaps by the time this book is published they will have changed.

STEWART GORE-BROWNE

APPENDIX II

MEMORANDUM ON THE REPRESENTATION OF AFRICANS AND OTHER RACES IN THE FEDERATION OF RHODESIA AND NYASALAND AND IN NORTHERN RHODESIA (1952)

The African people will accept nothing short of full adult franchise, with no reserved seats or other special safeguards for minority groups, as the ultimate means of electing Legislåtive Assemblies and Councils with sovereign authority in the Federation and in Northern Rhodesia. They agree to advance to this by steps that remain within the bounds of practice and constituted politics, and progressively improve the representation of Africans. Each step shall not be so long delayed that the adults of today cannot foresee the ultimate realization of the ideal in their own lifetime. Steps foreseen as temporarily acceptable are:

(i) Communal rolls with a fixed number of seats for each racial group.

(ii) A common roll with reservation of a fixed minimum number of seats for minority groups.

A balance of power in the hands of official members would be acceptable in the early stages as long as there were Africans among the officials.

The reform of the Territorial Constitution to be carried out in 1958 is dealt with first.

Territorial Constitution.

The present distribution of seats in the *Legislative Council* is: 4 Africans (recommended to the Governor by the African Representative Council), 2 Europeans representing African Interests (nominated by the Governor), 12 Elected members (Elected by a roll of 12,000 European voters and about 3 Africans), 8 Official members (ex officio or appointed by the Governor. All are Europeans), making a total of 26. The Speaker is nominated.

Proposed redistribution of seats in 1958.

12 Africans (elected on separate African adult franchise roll), 12 elected by British subjects, 4 Official members (nominated by the Governor), making a total of 28. The Speaker to be chosen by the Members from outside the Council.

ZAMBIA SHALL BE FREE

Transitional Voters' Roll.

The first electoral roll for Africans can be the Native Tax Register. Every male taxpayer may obtain a vote to be cast by a female voter until a register of African adult females is drawn up. Any British subject or British Protected person may stand for election by Africans. It is conceivable that corruption or inefficiency may so damage the reputation of members that Africans may wish to elect members of another race. This should be allowed for in the constitution. The members elected by British subjects shall be elected on the present voters' rolls. No African who is a British subject shall vote for a candidate nominated as an African candidate.

Territorial Executive Council.

There are already 4 official members of the Executive Council as well as the Governor who are all pledged to act without discrimination against Africans and it is useless to nominate another European member to represent African interests, who has not the confidence of the African people, but gives to a thoroughly undemocratic Council a pretended African representation. The only thing acceptable to Africans is the nomination to the Executive Council of the African members of the Legislative Council chosen by all African members of the Legislative Council. There shall be as many African members of the Executive Council as there are unofficials elected by British subjects. Consideration should be given to nominating African official members to the Executive Council.

British Protected Persons.

Africans strongly object to the necessity of becoming British subjects before they can become full citizens of their own country. They consider it to be ridiculous that this extra citizenship should be made obligatory before they are given full voting rights. While they realize the benefit of membership of the Commonwealth for their country, they believe that citizenship of .Northern Rhodesia should carry Commonwealth citizen rights as it does in the Dominions and in Nigeria and the Gold Coast. This conception of citizenship must be accepted by the Government and then put into action by the formation of a common voters' roll based on adult franchise.

Common voters' roll and reserved seats for minorities.

It is acceptable to Africans that a certain number of seats in the Legislative Council shall be reserved for minority groups during the first years of elections by a common voters' roll. This will give the minority groups a feeling of security. It is foreseen that the political division of the people will not always be by race. As an African class of wealthy property owners and high salaried workers develops they will find their interests to be closer to those of the European and Asian monied classes, while European and Asian working men will see their interests allied to the African workers. When no race any longer has reason to fear domination by another race, the policy of reserved seats for minorities can be ended and the Legislative Council will be a truly democratic expression of the will of the majority of all citizens.

Reserved seats in the Legislative Council.

The system of reserved seats for minorities for a period during the transition to full democratic representation will be acceptable on the general principles laid down by W. J. M. Mackenzie in his recommendations for Tanganyika as they may be applied to a community with only two politically important racial divisions.

Change from Communal roll to Common roll.

It would be acceptable to Africans that the system of electing communal representatives on communal rolls should change to that of common representation on a common roll when the number of voters of each race are equal and the merging of the communal rolls into a common roll would give parity to the number of African voters and European (or British subject voters). This might not be considered as providing sufficient safeguard for the minorities if it came very soon, and a system of reserved seats for minorities is put forward later to lessen their fears.

Common roll with restricted franchise.

It has been strongly advocated by some who have the interests of the African people at heart that communal rolls and communal representation are likely to hinder advance to a genuine democracy. It is claimed by them that a common roll should be established by the addition of Africans who have some income, property or educational qualification.

If the franchise was extended to British Protected persons this would not be unacceptable to Africans if the qualifications were such that the number of Africans who could immediately become eligible should be equal to the European voters or enough to influence elections to a notable extent and that the administration of the tests should be in impartial hands.

Educational tests.

At present, the educational test is that the voter wishing to register should correctly fill in a form written in English (Schedule 1. Form A. of the Legislative Council Ordinance Cap. 2. of the Laws of Northern Rhodesia and Section 12). If this form was available in the most widely spoken vernacular languages of Northern Rhodesia, this test would be acceptable to Africans for a transitional period.

Means Test.

The number of Africans occupying houses valued at £250 or

more is increasing rapidly. If this test was administered impartially it would be acceptable to Africans for a transitional period. (Cap. 2. Laws of Northern Rhodesia Section 11(a).) The income required has been fixed at a point attained by very few Africans but with the allowance of £50 for rations or housing reducing the requirements to £150 a year or £12 10 0 a month the number is increasing. Africans are afraid that European employers may dismiss Africans before they have completed a year's work at this wage in order that they may be disenfranchised. If it was sufficient to prove that £12 10 0 a month was earned in regular employment for three months in any year and if all forms of bonuses and additional emoluments were taken into consideration this test, administered impartially, would not be unacceptable to Africans as a transitional measure. (Cap. 2. Laws of Northern Rhodesia Section 11(c).)

Assessment and administration of tests.

A Board shall be established, if the formation of a common roll on these terms shall be decided on, which shall have as many Africans chosen by the African members of the Legislative Council on it as there are Europeans, whose duty it shall be to draw up and keep up to date the common electoral roll for the Territory. Appeals from this Board shall be heard in the same way as appeals from a Registering Office (Cap. 2. Laws of Northern Rhodesia First Schedule Section 6).

African Representatives in the Legislative Council.

The representation of African interests by Europeans has been made unacceptable to Africans by the record of the Europeans nominated. They have not identified themselves with the people they are supposed to represent. As they are not responsible to the African people and do not depend on them for re-election, this is not surprising. If African interests are to be represented by

Europeans, they should be Europeans elected by Africans. This also refers to representation on the Executive Council.

The Federal Assembly.

The African people wish to see the Federation, which was imposed on them in spite of their unanimous opposition, dissolved as soon as possible. Until this has been accomplished they wish to see its constitution develop progressively towards true democracy.

Representation in the Federal Assembly.

The present position is:

	N. Rhodesia	Nyasaland	S. Rhodesia
Africans chosen by Africans	2	2	–
Africans elected by Europeans	–	–	2
Europeans representing Africans	1	1	1
Elected by British subjects	8	4	14
Total	11	7	17
Grand Total	35		

The total number of Africans eligible to vote as British subjects is under 500. There are over 50,000 European voters.

Recommendations are made for the number of seats allocated to Nyasaland and Southern Rhodesian representatives because the principles involved are common to all three Territories. They are not necessarily accepted by Africans of those Territories.

Proposed re-allocation of seats in the Federal Assembly.

The seats were allocated in the constitution of 1953 on the basis of the importance of the European populations of the

Territories and the financial influence of those Europeans.

This is unacceptable to Africans who can see no reason why the three Territories should not have equal representation. The influence of large European numbers in Southern Rhodesia and their tenure of half the land area, is countered by the influence of the great Northern Rhodesian copper industry and by the greater African population of Nyasaland. These things cannot be weighed and assessed with numerical accuracy. Parity of representation is the only fair system. It is proposed that each Territory sends 12 members to the Federal Assembly.

Representation of Africans in the Federal Assembly.

The common roll in Southern Rhodesia is an inoperative force that accords no proper representation to Africans. Until such time as the Southern Rhodesian common roll and common rolls in Northern Rhodesia and Nyasaland are political realities, there should be communal representation for Africans for the election of their own members.

Parity of Representation.

As a transitional measure, Africans would accept a Federal Assembly consisting of 6 Africans and 6 Europeans (or persons elected by the British subjects) for each Territory.

Proposal.

	N. Rhodesia	Nyasaland	S. Rhodesia
Elected by African Roll	6	6	6
Elected by Europeans or British subjects	6	6	6
Total	12	12	12
Grand Total	36		

Reserved Seats in Southern Rhodesia.

If it is thought inadvisable to split the common roll of Southern Rhodesia, the election could be carried on on the basis of six reserved seats for those African candidates who obtained most votes. It is realized that this system perpetuates the present indefensible system whereby representatives of Africans are elected by a roll on which there is an overwhelming number of Europeans, and that African candidates if they are to have any chance of success have to obtain the endorsement of a European political party. The alternative is put forward here because Southern Rhodesian political organizations may prefer to fight for a fairer common roll than for a transitional period with communal rolls. This does not by any means suggest a separate communal roll system in Southern Rhodesia which does not now exist.

The African Affairs Board.

The African Affairs Board has not been an effective check on discriminating legislation in the Federation. The Income Tax Act which made the Africans of Northern Rhodesia and Nyasaland liable for income tax for the first time without relieving them of Territorial Native Tax, and the Cadet Corps Act which excluded Africans by implication from its scope, passed unopposed. This was not unexpected as the numbers of Africans and Europeans on the Board was equal while the Chairman was, and still is, a European nominated by a Governor and not chosen by Africans. The African Affairs Board should be altered so that Africans representing African interests alone remain on it and those chosen by Africans (and not as in Southern Rhodesia by a European electorate) shall be in a majority. The Governor-General should be instructed to appoint a Secretary to the Board whose duty it would be to point out to the members any point in proposed legislation that might in any way come within the scope of its constitutional powers. It is suggested that the Secretary should be an African from outside the Board.

Democratic Government the Ultimate Aim.

Any move towards Dominion status or government in-dependent of the United Kingdom is opposed without reserve by all Africans. In putting forward this memorandum as a declaration of a policy acceptable to the African people of Northern Rhodesia, it is necessary to repeat that each step pro-posed is acceptable only in that it leads towards the democratic government of Northern Rhodesia as a Territory and, so long as the present Federal constitution is effective, as part of the Federa-tion. Africans have no power to bring about the change they ask for by constitutional means, as they are excluded from the franchise and are inadequately represented in the councils and assemblies. The Secretary of State is reminded that he can use his official votes in the Executive and Legislative Councils of Northern Rhodesia to bring about the changes asked for by Africans. If he does not do so the responsibility of driving Africans, in their fear and despair, to take unconstitutional steps to amend the constitution will rest with him.

In Federal matters, the constitution so strongly endorsed by a Conservative government makes direct action by the government of the United Kingdom almost impossible. The government of the United Kingdom will be, under Article 99 of the Federal constitution, a party to the conference to be convened between 1960 and 1962 to consider amendments to the constitution. With the control of the Territorial delegations from Northern Rhodesia and Nyasaland the United Kingdom can exert very strong pressure at this conference. The Secretary of State is requested to show now that he will be prepared at the conference to use his influence to effect amendments to the constitution that will give more fair play to Africans. In that way he may be able to lessen the great anxiety and bitterness of the African people, and render unnecessary action beyond the scope of the constitution to which they might be driven if all hope of reassurance was lost.

The demands for a united government, Dominion status and

apartheid by European settlers are wholly unacceptable to Africans and any tendency by the United Kingdom government to give way to any one of these demands will be met with opposition which may break into unpleasant happenings.

APPENDIX III

COMMENTS ON THE PROPOSALS FOR CONSTITUTIONAL CHANGE IN NORTHERN RHODESIA (1958)

Historical

1 We wish to remind the British Government that our lands and people were entrusted by agreement with our forbears to the protection of Her Majesty's Government in the United Kingdom.
2 Northern Rhodesia came under the administration of the British Government in 1924 when it was declared a Protectorate by the Crown. Although the official policy was that of paramountcy of African interests, the protected persons were not represented at all in the Legislative Council for twenty-one years, yet the handful of Europeans who were then in the country were given adequate representation right away.
3 Africans were represented for the first time in 1938 indirectly when a European member was nominated by the Governor to represent them. At this time, there were 16 members in the Legislative Council which was made up as follows:

Official members (including the Governor as President
of the Council) 8
Unofficial members representing Europeans only............ 7
A European nominated to represent African interests...... 1
                                                                                    ——
                                                                                    16
                                                                                    ——

4 It was not until 1948 that Africans had some kind of 'direct' representation when 2 African members were appointed to the Legislative Council in addition to 2 Europeans nominated to represent African interests.

5 On the other hand, there was a corresponding increase of one in the official representation and two elected European members. The result of this was that the number of elected European members was equal for the first time to that of Official members, making the composition of the Legislative Council thus:

Official members (all white)	10
Unofficial members (representing the white settler element	10
White nominees to represent Africans	2
Appointed African members	2
	24

6 The next stage in this development came in 1954 when the number of appointed 'African representatives was increased to four with another corresponding increase in European representation and also a reduction in official representation, thus giving the vocal white settler element a majority in the Council, as shown below:

Official members (all white)	8
Unofficial members (representing the white settler element	12
White nominees to represent Africans	2
Appointed African members	4
	26

7 Sight must not be lost of the fact mentioned above that para-

mountcy of African interests was the official policy of Northern Rhodesia from 1924. This meant that when and if the interests of the Africans conflicted with those of the immigrant races, the interests of the Africans would prevail. This was a thorn in the flesh of the white settlers because on major issues the Colonial Office were prone to listen more to the Africans than to the settlers. A case in point was the insistent demand by the settlers to amalgamate the Rhodesias, which was turned down several times until the policy of African paramountcy was changed.

8 It must be placed on record that there was absolute treachery in the replacement of the policy of paramountcy of African interests by the woolly one of partnership. When this change took place, the consent of the Chiefs and their people was not even sought. Instead, in 1948 two hand-picked Africans were flown to London in the company of top Government officials and elected European representatives to dismantle the policy of African Paramountcy.

9 The so-called partnership policy remained undefined until 1954 when the Moffat Resolutions were passed in the Legislative Council. The first indication as to the meaning of 'Partnership' as conceived by the European representatives was when Mr Roy Welensky, leader of the white settler representatives, said in the Legislative Council in 1952, during the debate on the Federal Scheme, that not all partnerships were 'fifty-fifty', thus replacing the old paramountcy policy by one of European paramountcy.

10 Up to now the jealously guarded Executive Council has been the prerogative of the Government officials and European representatives. Since 1948, one of the white nominees representing African interests has been sitting in the Council, but it was not until 1954 that a portfolio was offered to him. It must be recorded here that these so-called African representatives have never had the confidence of the Africans.

Principles of Constitutional Change

11 We appreciate the principle contained in Para. 16 of the White Paper that 'Political parties should begin to develop on non-racial lines and that politics should cut straight across race'. Government say that they have consistently followed this policy and they believe that this policy has always been generally accepted by the people in Northern Rhodesia. Government have supported this line of policy by quoting the Moffat Resolutions. The relevant Resolutions are (1) and (2) which read:

(1) The objective of policy in Northern Rhodesia must be to remove from each race the fear that the other might dominate for its own racial benefit and to move forward from the present system of racial representation in the territorial legislature towards a franchise with no separate representation for the races.

(ii) Until that objective can be fully achieved a period of transition will remain during which special arrangements in the Legislative and Executive Councils must continue to be made so as to ensure that no race can use either the preponderance of its members or its more advanced stage of development to dominate the other for its own racial benefit.

12 The following extract from the Moffat Resolutions demands special attention: 'That no race can use either the preponderance of its numbers or its more advanced stage of development to dominate the other for its own racial benefit'. It would appear from this that the best solution to our constitutional problem now would be parity of representation in the Legislative Council between Africans and Europeans. Government, however, who are themselves committed to the Moffat Resolutions argue in the White Paper that parity of representation between the races 'could not but consolidate and perpetuate a racial outlook'.

13 Using that argument Government have gone on to make pro-

posals which are almost identical with the recommendations of the United Federal Party which give the European minority in this country a big majority over African members. It is quite safe to assume from this that the reason given by the Government against parity is a false one intended to support the Government case for proposing a constitution which gives the Europeans control of Government because of their 'more advanced stage of development to dominate over the Africans for their own racial benefit'.

14 It must be noted that whereas His Excellency started having constitutional discussions early in 1957 with individual members and groups of members of the Legislative Council and others, it was not until February 1958 that he met the leaders of the African National Congress. It is quite evident that when His Excellency met Congress leaders he had already irrevocably committed himself to accepting almost *in toto* the proposals of the settlers.

15 We note the Government's desire that 'the constitutional arrangements should ensure that the government of the country will continue to rest in the hands of responsible men, men with understanding and of sufficient education and experience of affairs to be able to reason and to exercise judgment between alternative courses of action'. So much depends on the definition of the word 'responsible'! As could be instanced from the White Paper, a 'responsible' person may be only a rich man with a knowledge of advanced English!

16 Government wishes that 'the electoral system must encourage the return of men or women who are prepared and indeed disposed to consider and balance the interests of all racial groups, and who are prompted primarily by a spirit of public service to the whole community'. To get these men the White Paper proposes to set the qualification for franchise so high that the mass of Africans will not be able to qualify, thus defeating Government's own objective 'that no one race can use either the preponderance of its numbers or its more advanced stage of development'.

17 Government intends to discourage the return of extremists who, it claims, would look to sectional interests. It is no secret that in Government circles extremists are either Dominion Party followers or African National Congress members. There is nothing to bar Dominion Party followers from either qualifying as voters or standing as candidates. On the other hand, the majority of Africans would be left without a vote because Government fears that if a substantial number of them were enfranchised they would be misused by the so-called extremists.

18 Government would like to label the African National Congress extremist. It goes without saying that Congress represents ninety-nine per cent of the African political opinion which means, therefore, that all Congress members are extremists and therefore most Africans are extremists. If and when extremism becomes a common character trait, then it ceases to be extremism. Therefore, whether they like it or not, Government must enfranchise the Africans as they must have people of their own political thought to represent them in the Legislative Council, and the Executive Council for that matter.

19 Government proposes to 'give the vote to those who are contributing to the wealth and welfare of the country and who are capable of exercising it with judgment and public spirit'. Judging from Government's definition of a responsible person referred to above, it follows here that when they propose to limit the franchise to people who are contributing to the wealth and welfare of the country and others, they mean the European settlers in this country.

20 We contend that the African contributes much more than his white boss. The African has contributed blood on the battlefield in defence of the British Empire; the African has contributed to the wealth of this country by providing cheap labour and by paying poll tax and other forms of taxation, direct or indirect and now including income tax. Over and above that the African has provided the land.

21 In view of all this, we believe the African has a strong case

for demanding a much better franchise than the one proposed. In our opinion, and in the name of democracy, it should be universal adult franchise based on ONE MAN ONE VOTE.

22 Government have rejected the concept of universal adult suffrage as unsuitable for Northern Rhodesia, simply because the Tredgold Franchise Commission rejected it as unsuitable for Southern Rhodesia.

23 By refusing the Congress proposal of universal adult suffrage based on ONE MAN ONE VOTE and adopting the Tredgold Commission recommendations on Southern Rhodesia, it does reveal the idea behind the scheme. It is now quite obvious that the Secretary of State wishes to see a complete constitutional link between the two Rhodesias with a view to bringing about amalgamation of the Rhodesias probably in 1960 when the Federal Constitution comes up for review.

24 The Federal Constitution says that there shall not be amalgamation at any future time but it can now be seen that the entrenched clause is *de facto* being flouted.

25 This shows just how meaningless British guarantees and promises are, however entrenched they may be. If this is the plot of the Colonial Office against the Africans in Northern Rhodesia we can only say this, that we are heading for disaster.

26 In the White Paper the seats in the Legislative Council are divided between black and white and there can be no question whatsoever of Africans swamping Europeans.

27 We do not agree that the best way to give Africans a proper measure of representation in the House would be to adopt a qualitative franchise. On the contrary, we believe that the best way to do this would be to give parity of representation in the House as well as universal adult franchise based on ONE MAN ONE VOTE.

28 While we are diametrically opposed to any form of a qualitative franchise we must make these remarks in passing. Government have proposed to award the vote to educated Chiefs on their own right and also to educated headmen, hereditary

182

councillors, pensioners and ministers of religion.

29 There are 853 Chiefs and important headmen in Northern Rhodesia, and from a personal knowledge of most of them we estimate that of these not more than 100 would be likely to qualify. The rest who have not got the necessary literacy qualification would not.

30 Another point for Government to note is that it is not money that makes a responsible person. Government have, by awarding the Chiefs the vote, agreed that the Chiefs, despite their poverty, do responsible work. It is, therefore, not fair to exclude a person from voting simply because he does not have the means qualification.

Congress Proposals

31 We agree with Government when they say that Northern Rhodesia has not yet advanced to the stage where the colour of their members is of no concern of the electorate, whether that electorate be predominantly black or white. We note also that Government does realize that however much they may wish to have non-racial representation it is just not feasible and shall never be in a society like ours under the present set-up. Indeed, however much they may wish to have non-racial representation it is just not feasible and shall never be in a society like ours under the present set-up. Indeed, however much we kid ourselves in terms of non-racialism, none of us shall forget the shade of his skin.

32 However, during the transitory period i.e., from now to 1964, we commend this scheme to the Secretary of State for the Colonies, for his consideration:

A Speaker appointed by the Governor, 35 Elected Members, 21 Elected Africans, 14 Elected Europeans and 7 Nominated Officials, making 21 African Members and 21 European Members.

33 As regards the Executive Council, the African National Con-

gress proposes: the Governor as President, 3 African Elected Members, 3 European Elected Members and 3 European Officials. This gives the Europeans a majority of 7 in the Executive Council.

34 While it may be true that the bulk of the African population resides in the rural areas covered by the six special constituencies it is a fact that along the line of rail where Africans are only given two representatives there are, according to the alleged figures quoted in Appendix B of the White Paper, 17,295 probable voters as against 7,353 in the rural areas.

35 It is therefore completely illogical to give 7,353 voters six representatives and 17,295 voters only two, just because they happen to live in the 'Ordinary' 12 constituencies where the interests of the Europeans are predominant.

36 It is quite true, however, that the bulk of Europeans reside along the line of rail and this is borne out by the figures quoted in the White Paper.

37 It is provided that every 'special' candidate standing for election should be required to obtain a certificate from two-thirds of the Chiefs recognized by the Governor in his constituency that those Chiefs have no objection to his standing as a candidate. The certificate, it is proposed, should be signed in the presence of witnesses duly appointed by the Governor.

38 Government believes that because local government in the towns is already closely linked with the territorial centre of Government and the Legislative Council, a similar link should be forged between the Legislative Council and the Native Authorities in the rural areas. They propose most strangely that the best way to do this is by using the above ridiculous method.

39 In fact, this method does not bear any semblance at all to the link the Municipalities have with Central Government. A similar link would be to propose that every European candidate in an Ordinary constituency should obtain a certificate signed in the presence of a number of witnesses duly appointed by the Governor, from two-thirds of the municipal councillors in his

constituency that those councillors had no objection to his standing as a candidate – imagining that all such councillors held
remunerative office under the Crown.

40 There are three main reasons against this proposal. The first
is that this proposal if adopted can quite easily be misused by
Chiefs and the witnesses appointed by the Governor. While we
have no idea as to what type of people will be nominated as
witnesses, it is quite possible that Chiefs and the witnesses might
belong to certain political parties. Party loyalty could easily make
these people fail to execute their work without bias.

41 The second reason against this proposal is that it discriminates
against African candidates standing for special constituencies and
makes their initial work very difficult.

42 The final and most important reason against this proposal is
that, if passed, it will give the Governor power to dictate who to
nominate for election to the Legislative Council.

43 This is a most wicked provision which has no parallel in any
known democratic country. To accept this would be tanta-
mount to accepting direct dictatorship and despotism.

44 In conclusion, the African National Congress would like to
draw the attention of the Secretary of State for the Colonies to
the fact that the African National Congress plan for parity of
representation is more than supported by the Government's own
figures in Appendix B of the White Paper.

45 It is noted that the 18,886 Ordinary voters in the 12 Constituencies along the line of rail have 12 European representatives.
On that basis the 17,295 special voters on the line of rail have a
legitimate claim for 11 representatives.

46 On the other hand, the 1,126 Ordinary voters in the rural areas
of the Protectorate have been offered two representatives. Working on the same proportion of representation again, the 7,353
mainly African voters are entitled to 13 representatives instead
of the 6 as proposed by Government.

47 On that basis there would be 24 African members in the Legis-

lative Council as against the 21 the African Congress has asked
for.

H. M. NKUMBULA.　　　　　　　K. D. KAUNDA.
National President.　　　　　　National Secretary.
For, and on behalf of, The National Executive Council of the
African National Congress of Northern Rhodesia.

APPENDIX IV

REPORT ON THE DISTURBANCES IN GWEMBE VALLEY, PRESENTED
TO THE AFRICAN NATIONAL CONGRESS ON 14 DECEMBER 1953
(Unedited, to preserve authenticity)

For many years the people in the Gwembe Valley and district
have been suffering from Government oppressive laws. These
disturbances were more accentuated with the introduction of the
African National Congress in the area.

In the month of May 1953 there came strangers at Chief
Simamba's village. These men were Mr Simon Mambo (District
Organizing Secretary for African National Congress) and another
man whose name we do not know. The Chief sent out his
Kapasus or Messengers to tell all the people that on the following day there would be a meeting. All the people in the Chief's
area went to the meeting on the appointed day, and we were
also there. Whilst the messengers were spreading the news about
this meeting, at Siakumbeni's village they found a man of the
Gwembe Native Authority to visit them. When he saw that
people were rejoicing, he queried what they hoped the Congress
would do for them. The people answered that they were only
glad because Congress men had come to their area to see for
themselves and from their lips they could hear the deplorable
conditions under which they lived. This was considered an insult and a man and his mother were instantly arrested and handcuffed.

At the meeting Mr Simon Mambo started by saying, 'The

Europeans usually tell us that there is freedom in this country; yet there is no freedom. A man and his mother were arrested yesterday because of saying that they were glad to hear that Congress members were in this part of the country – there is then no freedom of speech. We, the Africans, are troubling other Africans. But if we unite in the name of the Northern Rhodesia African Congress, trouble would be less because every man would know what was wrong and what was right towards his fellow men.'

Mr Mambo asked Chief Simamba what was worrying them most. The Chief said: (i) compulsory planting of cassava, and not being allowed to eat same before Government says so; and (ii) *Nzembwe* or collective storage of kaffir corn leaving some families starving; and (iii) compulsory digging of rubbish or refuse pits; and (iv) forced labour recruitment. Mr Mambo then asked the Chief (Simamba) whether Congress is acceptable. The Chief asked what was Congress? Mr Mambo said that Congress was the political unity of all the people so that if possible they might find a way out of some of the illegitimate and unnecessary sufferings, a way out of slavery, a way to peace. 'At present, any day the District Commissioner likes, a Chief may be deposed from his birth-right of Chieftainship.' Chief Simamba said that Congress was acceptable. Mr Mambo then said, 'My brethren, our organization needs money. If this great task is to be carried out, those of you who have accepted can come forward and donate money.' Chief Simamba was the first to donate two pounds and ten shillings (£2 10 0). Then the Chief told (us) his people to donate also for he had himself donated. Then the village Headmen started donating. Each according to his wish from 2/- to 5/- per person. Then we also started donating, each man a shilling (1/-). All of us who donated received receipts.

After this, we all sat down and the meeting continued. Mr Simon Mambo asked if amongst ourselves there was anybody who could write so that he could be a secretary to enrol new members and receive donations from members of the community. So people were elected for this work and these are their names: Chief Simamba, Siakumbila, a Chief's Councillor, Kwaipa, Mateyo, all of these four members were elected office-bearers for southern area. The others were Tebulu, and one other for the south-western area. These collected the money and put it together and this is the money which was taken to a Congress meeting at Chongo in the month of May.

On their return, the people who attended the Chongo meeting told us of the deliberations of that Conference but were sorry to hear that Chief Simamba after attending for a day went to attend a Government meeting at Mazabuka. We were also asked to donate more money. All the people or most of them donated, and this money was handed to Congress at a meeting held at Changa in Chief Sinadambwe's area. Mr Harry Nkumbula was there.

We told Mr Nkumbula of our sufferings, especially the forced cheap labour recruitment, forced planting of cassava 'which we are not being allowed to eat'. He (Mr Nkumbula) said that he did not know that the law of this country could allow that kind of human torture, and that when he returned to town he would interview some big Government Officials and ask if they knew that such a thing was going on in the Gwembe District. We went back to our villages after the meeting. We stayed peacefully for only one month and after that there came two Boma Messengers and one Kapasu from the Native Authority. They started arresting people for forced cheap labour, but at our villages we refused and no one was taken at that time. Then the Messengers talked about *Nzembwe* (collective storage of food), then the people refused (*pele bantu bakaka*) because of starvation after a family has put all their food into *Nzembwe*. And they did so because if anyone failed to bring food for such kind of storage he was to be arrested and fined at the Chief's Court. Chief Simamba said, 'It is Harry Nkumbula who had stopped you from obeying this order'.

After that the party left for Siakumbeni's village where they slept. There we heard that they talked of the same matter but the Headman and his people refused to be bluffed by the Messengers, and there were no more people to be arrested for forced labour for most of them had already been arrested in the past few days. Then on the following day the Messengers left for Chafukwa's village. They asked Headman Chafukwa to accompany them to Chief Simamba's village, on account of his few remaining peoples' refusal to go for forced labour and disobeying *Nzembwe* Orders or Regulations passed by the Native Authority. The Headman refused. Then they told him that it was not he whom they wanted. They said that they had come specially for 'this Congress member' – pointing at Simon.

Simon said: 'They asked for my *Situpa* (Identification Certificate), but I declined to give them this because they did not tell me what my charge was. Chief Simamba was also present, three other village-mates and I were handcuffed at the spot and were told that we were to be taken away for (*Chibalo*) forced labour. We were at first taken to Chief Simamba's village, and were handcuffed as we followed the party round about in the villages where the party was still looking for other people. The Headmen of our villages followed us on the following day. We were going towards the concentration camps when we met these Headmen on the way. The Headmen asked the Messengers what offence we had committed so as to be handcuffed. The Headmen asked them if at all we had not paid our Poll Tax. The Messengers failed to give an answer, and instead they handed over the keys to the Headmen so that they could unlock the handcuffs and gave us our *Situpas* and said to the Headmen, "There are your men". There was no trouble. All was said and done amicably and without violence. We went back to our villages and stayed peacefully without trouble for at least one month. After that the District Commissioner came with his four Messengers and asked where Headman Chafukwa was. They ordered me to sit down and asked me to clap hands for them. I did all what they ordered me to do and likewise I was ordered to take him to Chilimanzi's village.'

Headman Chilimanzi stated: 'When they arrived, they ordered six of us to sit down and to stretch our legs, and later ordered us to clap our hands. We did as ordered for we were told that that was the kind of an honour a white man ought to be given. After that we were taken to our cassava gardens and when we reached the gate of the fence of the gardens we were again told to sit down and stretch our legs as we did in the village and to clap our hands for the District Commissioner. We did as ordered and instructed. Some of the cassava had been eaten. We were asked as to who ate the cassava. We answered and said that monkeys eat the cassava for they raided the gardens every day. The interpreters were Chief Simamba himself and Head Messenger Chimputu. They said that it was Harry Nkumbula who has told the monkeys to eat the cassava. But I said that long before we heard of Harry Nkumbula from other people, monkeys have been raiding our gardens, and I for one usually buy cassava from other people to plant or replace those eaten by monkeys. Chief Simamba said that I was telling a lie, and that I had eaten the cassava. But I said that I certainly was not a monkey. After that we were all taken to Chafukwa's village where together with people at Chafukwa's village we were told to sit down and to clap hands for the white man, and we did so. Then the District Commissioner through an interpreter spoke and asked Simon as to who had eaten the cassava.'

Simon stated: 'I said that it was the monkeys that ate it. Then the District Commissioner asked me and said, "Have the monkeys got hoes?". And I said that the hoes were used at the time of planting the cassava. Then Chief Simamba said: "You should not eat cassava any more for you have already accepted the African Congress of Harry Nkumbula.' Then we were told to stand up and go back to the village. We were not allowed to enter the village. We were shown where to go by the point (indication) of a finger towards the road where a Government lorry awaited for us.'

Headman Chilimanzi stated: 'I asked what the lorry had to do with us for if you have come to see cassava, you should go round all the villages and see what the monkeys have done with the cassava. I was then held by the head and violently pushed towards the lorry. They encircled us and pushed us to the lorry. I could not tolerate it for I had a wound on my right shin, so I asked what crime we had committed which made them to push us as they did. I was shouted at with an insult, "You will be beaten today." Seeing that the people who wanted to beat us had four rifles with them we wondered what kind of beating that would be and, therefore, we scattered and ran away. Then they returned in the village of Chafukwa. Chief Simamba warned the women in the village saying, "Your husbands who have joined the Congress should be careful for the Government is determined to torture them until they can denounce Congress." Then in the ears of the women who were in the village, through an interpreter, a Messenger, the District Commissioner and the Chief talked of the possibility of bringing down Police management and soldiers "to fix these people". They left Chafukwa's village and went easterly to Simangilile; on the way they met a man herding goats. His name is Chisenga the deputy to Headman Simangilile. They called for him and when he was come they ordered him to sit down and when he was sat they surrounded him. Chief Simamba said to him, "This is the new District Commissioner, so clap your hands for him." After clapping his hands he was ordered to mount on to the lorry. He asked what he was going to do up in the lorry. They got hold of him and handled him firmly into the lorry and drove off towards Chief Simamba's village. On the way, they met a man on a push bicycle and Chisenga asked this man to convey the message to Simangilile's village to go and tell his people that they had stolen him by a white man. When the villagers heard about it they went to Simamba's village to find out. They found that another man was also arrested. His name is Headman Chingwemyuka. Chief Simamba was looking after them because the

District Commissioner had gone to Chirundu Road. The people waited for the District Commissioner until they were so hungry so that they left for their villages; together with them were the two alleged culprits. When the District Commissioner returned from the Chirundu Road on the following day, he asked the Chief where the two arrested people were. He was told that they had gone back to their homes. Then the District Commissioner went back to Gwembe Boma.

'After one week there came four lorries full of African Constables with but three Europeans, together with the District Commissioner. When they reached Simangilile's village, they started chasing after women. They found six women with baskets of kaffir corn on their heads and this was spilt when they tried to rescue themselves from this sudden and unexpected attack by policemen they had never seen before. But they were arrested or captured. When the boys who were herding goats saw that, they ran to the river and when the men started homewards to see what had happened, on the way they met this gang of policemen armed with rifles chasing for them. The men started running away. Chisenga particularly continued to run up to the river when he was told that if he would swim across they would fire at him. Therefore he returned towards them and was arrested and handcuffed, and they took him to Chief Simamba.

'When we heard of it all the people of the village on our side gathered together so that the "Impi" of policemen should find us together in the village. On the day that followed at about nine o'clock, the Messengers and Constables were armed with rifles and sticks; when they gave a sound of alarm, we realized what was coming on us and we all ran away. We were followed. The Messenger who was very cross and running after us asked why we were running away. We told him that we were afraid "because you have come well-armed and staged a war on us, though unarmed as we are. You have come with many policemen with rifles and it can never be anything less than war." The District Commissioner sent a Messenger to inform us that he had come with policemen and rifles to show us that "the Government has power to kill you if you refuse Government laws". We said that we did not want the District Commissioner and the policemen to come near to us for he had come to fight us. Then he sent the Messenger for the second time to tell us that the District Commissioner was prepared to hide the policemen somewhere while he would be talking to us. We agreed to this but we were suspicious of being trapped and killed by the hidden policemen while we talked with the District Commissioner. But when we saw how he pleaded and persuaded us for quite a while, we decided to meet him. When we met him, he talked to us through Messenger Chimpuku's interpretation saying that he had come with the armed police to show us "Government has power to force anybody to obey Government laws however bad or good they may be. The Congress members are not allowed in Gwembe area now because they have made the people to reason and that's why we have banned them to appear in this area. Anybody who will be found to be a Congress member will be arrested."

'We replied that "although you have banned Congress these laws have for long been unjust to us – and for such a long time for which we are not prepared to follow these – forced cheap labour, compulsory *Nzembwe* storage and cassava planting". Then the District Commissioner and the policemen returned back to Gwembe Boma.

'After four days, there came eight lorries and one jeep all full of policemen armed with rifles. We were sent for and all the people in Chief Simamba's area went there. The District Commissioner talked and said that he had brought this battalion to us to demonstrate and show how the Government was so powerful and what would befall those who resist Government Regulations however bad. "If you refuse to obey, you will perish of guns," he continued. "The Government knows that there are such laws as forced labour, *Nzembwe* and compulsory cassava plantation and its accompaniments. If you think I am lying to you, here is the District Commissioner from Lusaka who will confirm my statement." Then the so-called District Commissioner from Lusaka said that we all know about these laws.

'We told them that "we are against cassava plantation because if the monkeys eat the cassava we are to be fined six pounds (£6 0 0). And if anyone refused to go for the forced cheap labour he is sent to prison."

'The District Commissioner said that "Congress has no right to tell you what is a bad law or a good law, therefore you should obey all the laws". We told him that we had already accepted the Congress, "for in other areas although there is Congress, or no Congress, there is no more forced labour, and we are determined to remain Congress members".

'After the meeting, he told us that he would be coming to our homes on the following day. On that appointed day, we were gathered in Chilimanzi's village and the District Commissioner came with the other said District Commissioner from Lusaka, the Head Messenger and a Boma Clerk who interpreted for him and he asked what we thought about these things. We told him that we wanted that the Government should be buying food from us so that in the time of hunger, those who happen to starve could buy the food from the Government, and that we were not prepared to be forced for cheap labour. But he only asked us as to who had given us such a sense of reasoning. We told him that it was because of suffering for many years which we have seen ourselves. Then he asked to find out who were the Congress members, but nobody came forward. Then he said he would look for them for that was why he had brought the police with him. He said he knew why we were talking as we did because of the meeting we had at Changa with Mr Nkumbula.

'For that reason, he said that this year he would make sure that we would not cultivate our gardens, because he would be raiding our villages and arresting the people for forced labour. However much we might hide he would bring enough policemen to look for us in our gardens for either forced labour or prison.

'On the following day the District Commissioner came again with the Chief and the Chief told us "I am telling you what the District Commissioner has told me to tell you and that is that Congress is an organization of fools and I do not want it". We told the District Commissioner that the Chief thinks Congress is no good because nobody forces him for cheap labour, but we say that we like the African National Congress. The District Commissioner and the Chief Simamba said that Congress members should be sent to jail.

'After this, there passed only one week before the police came and arrested twenty-one men of Simangilile's village. They were arrested at night. From that time up to this time, people do not sleep in their houses. They do not cultivate for fear of unexpected arrest.

'For this reason, and although the rain has come, we cannot cultivate our gardens for fear of being arrested, and, on our hearing that Congress members may not come because of the ban from entering Gwembe Valley, we have come to let you know of the torture in our land which you might not know of. And also to ask if it is possible for us to interview some big Government Officials who just hear that people in Gwembe are bad, that if they hear from us the true facts, they may be persuaded to think otherwise and try to rectify the conditions at home. The Government has stopped us from cultivating in Gwembe because of the reasons already given and there is a danger of a famine in the coming year.

'When we complain about bad conditions to our Chief, he threatens and warns us of being sent to jail so we are afraid.

'That is all we have got to say.

'We are,

Headman Chilimanzi. Headman Chatugwa. Manyengela. Simon Siavima. Edward Simunyama. Samson Simamba. Mackison Sibakwi. Samuel Magayi Chafukwa.'

On 18 December, four days after the report was presented to Congress, I wrote to the Secretary for Native Affairs, Lusaka:

Re: GWEMBE DISTURBANCES

Sir,

With reference to our conversation this morning, I must say how sorry we are for your refusal to have an interview with us on the above subject.

You are aware, as I pointed out to you, that the Government has made certain allegations against the Congress about the Gwembe incident and it is my duty to clear up the situation.

I told you there are at my office here in Lusaka eight men who have fled away from the bad Native Administration under some of your Officers which is rife there. These men desired to see you in person and air their grievances to you as the head of the Native Affairs. It is most regrettable that you offer these people no opportunity of seeing you.

As you will notice from the enclosed narrative of their problems it is out of the question to ask them to see their District Commissioner. They simply wouldn't go near him. They fear him because of the things he has done to them. Let us hope for God's sake that these poor people will not be tortured the more for looking up to Congress in their difficult times when they go back to their homes.

I must here affirm in the strongest terms that this African National Congress has nothing to do with the Gwembe disturbances. The mismanagement of their affairs by your Department has led to the trouble. We, as Congress, would not accept any blame by Government because of its own maladministration. We have pledged ourselves to a policy of non-co-operation in matters detrimental to African interests, without violence. This we mean to follow up to a point where it shall prove beneficial to the people concerned.

I am,
Sir
Yours faithfully,
K. D. Kaunda

Index to Text

Index to Appendices